FOR GOD SO LOVED THE WORLD

FOR GOD SO LOVED THE WORLD

…and everyone in it

Tiffany Root
and
Kirk VandeGuchte

WEST BOW
P R E S S
A DIVISION OF THOMAS NELSON

WestBow Press books may be ordered through booksellers or by contacting:

WestBow Press
A Division of Thomas Nelson
1663 Liberty Drive
Bloomington, IN 47403
www.westbowpress.com
1-(866) 928-1240

Because of the dynamic nature of the Internet, any web addresses or links contained in this book may have changed since publication and may no longer be valid. The views expressed in this work are solely those of the author and do not necessarily reflect the views of the publisher, and the publisher hereby disclaims any responsibility for them.

Certain stock imagery © Thinkstock.
Any people depicted in stock imagery provided by Thinkstock are models, and such images are being used for illustrative purposes only.

ISBN: 978-1-4497-1640-0 (sc)
ISBN: 978-1-4497-1642-4 (hc)
ISBN: 978-1-4497-1641-7 (e)

Library of Congress Control Number: 2011927680

Printed in the United States of America

WestBow Press rev. date: 6/7/2011

All scripture is from the NIV, unless otherwise noted.

All emphasis (bold & underline) in Scripture quotations are the authors'.

For Kaylee, my firstborn. May the LORD bless you and keep you, make His face shine on you, and give you peace. May you be filled with the light of His presence and love Him with all your heart, soul, mind, and strength. May you walk in the Truth. I love you. – Mommy

Now set your heart and your soul to seek the LORD your God . . .
1 Chronicles 22:19a

ACKNOWLEDGEMENTS

We want to give all thanks to God for giving us the insight and understanding to write this book. It is certainly only because of Him that we have undertaken to write it, and we give all glory to Him.

We also want to thank our spouses for their kindness and understanding. Joe and Barb, you're the best! Thank you to Tiffany's children too as she spent many hours at the computer instead of playing games.

CONTENTS

INTRODUCTION

"But if you love those who love you, what credit is that to you?
For even sinners love those who love them." (Luke 6:32 NKJV)

D o you know that Jesus never asks us to do anything that He's not willing to do as well? Jesus tells us in the above passage from Luke to love those who do not love us. That is something our God does - He loves those who do not love Him. Amazing! The love of God is amazing!

The book you are about to read focuses on God's love for people and His desire to save mankind. Did you know that the God who created the universe, set the stars in place, and created you, wants a relationship with you? The whole purpose of creation is relationship. God desires an intimate relationship with you and with everyone else He has ever created. That's what this book is about. It's about the desire God has for intimacy with **you**.

When God created the world, sun, moon, and stars, etc., He created humankind in His image with a free will. This is a will to love Him or reject Him. The first humans, Adam and Eve, freely loved God and trusted Him. The Bible says that the Lord would come down and actually walk in the Garden of Eden with Adam in the cool of the day.

How awesome! It wasn't until the devil disguised himself as a serpent and made Eve question the motives of God, that sin entered the world.

Eve doubted God's motives when the devil told her that the reason God didn't want her and Adam to eat from the Tree of the Knowledge of Good and Evil was because then they would be like God, knowing good from evil. The devil frequently uses doubt and half truths to deceive us. Adam and Eve did indeed know good from evil after eating the forbidden fruit, but they did not become like God. They became more distant from God. They hid themselves from God because they realized they had done wrong and they realized they were naked. This was the start of the break in the intimacy God desires with mankind.

Some question why God would put the Tree of Knowledge of Good and Evil in the Garden of Eden if He knew they would eat from it. The answer is that God did not make robots. He made humans in His image and likeness, with the ability to choose to do good or evil. God had to make humans able to choose life or death, good or evil, obedience or disobedience, to love or not to love, so that our obedience and love would not be forced. If it were forced and chosen for us, where would the joy in that be?

It is important to know that God did not need to make man in order to feel loved. God is love. He is perfectly content with Himself. Even the angels have a will and can choose to obey and love or choose to disobey and not love, as is evidenced with the fall of Satan and those angels that followed him.

God chose to make mankind because of intimacy. That is what He desires. It is because God so loved the world (all He created), that He made a way to save us all, even after sin and death entered the world because of the choices of Adam and Eve. The first thing God did after confronting Adam and Eve in their sinfulness was to sacrifice an animal in order to clothe His precious children with the animal's skin. Wow!

The first sacrifice made was by God and the reason was to help His children. The sacrifice of animals in order to atone (make right) for the sins of mankind continued until a little over 2,000 years ago, when Jesus came to earth in the flesh.

This is where forgiveness and healing really begins. God gave His one and only Son, Jesus, to save sinners, and we're all sinners. Most of the world either doesn't even know or doesn't even care, yet Christ died for us all. God so desired the intimacy of those He created, that He sent His Son to pay the price for all of the sins of the world so that He would have ultimate authority and dominion. The Bible says that all things are now under the feet of Jesus and that every name must bow to the name of Jesus. This is God's Kingdom on Earth as it is in Heaven. This is the gospel we are supposed to be preaching. Jesus is the Word in flesh, and we are to bring His Kingdom to the earth through the Holy Spirit that lives in us.

God's Word brings freedom because it is ultimate Truth. And where there is Truth, there is Freedom. We are in bondage when we believe anything contrary to the Truth of God's Word. The following chapters explain freedom in knowing Christ died for the whole world and that each person has access to the Father, through Jesus Christ alone. There is no other way.

The Bible comes to life when the Holy Spirit breathes life into it, not before. When He does, we experience profound truth. When we read our Bibles, we need to have our spirits' open to what God has to say, and we need hearts that are searching for truth. Then we experience life and revelation as we read.

The sword of Christ is His very own words. We read that Jesus yields a double-edged sword. One edge is the truth by which we are saved, the other edge is the same word (truth) by which we are condemned. There is no middle ground; the lukewarm are not saved. Either we follow His

Word or we don't. Either we are fully committed or not. What we think doesn't really matter with regard to being saved. It's only by His way that it can happen, and we are not in a position to negotiate or change the rules. We only decide one way or the other – will we follow Him or not?

Take this journey with us as we delve into what it means that "God so loved the world."

CHAPTER 1

God Loves Us All

For God so loved the world that he gave his one and only Son, that whoever believes in him shall not perish but have eternal life. John 3:16

People need love to thrive. They need it to live, or they can die. The following is a quote from an organization called Touch is Great.

Arguably, it was not until the appearance of the clinical reports by Dr. Rene Spitz (1945, 1947) that the seeds of research in the field of touch were sown. Spitz's reports reflect his anguished quest for a solution to the unexplainable deaths and pathologies of infants and toddlers in his care. The diagnosis of that era for these terminal children was "marasmus" (translation - "the withering away and dying of no apparent cause.") Spitz finally discovered that medicine, good nutrition, and clean surroundings impacted not the least on the tragic outcome. Only what Harry Harlow (1958, 1962) was to later call "contact comfort" turned out to be the "cure" for the excruciating deaths of these children. Touch deprivation is probably most damaging to an infant because, unlike the other four senses, the neonate has an extremely small amount of control over somatosensory self-stimulation due to underdeveloped motor control capacities. (http://www.touchisgreat.com/pb/wp_0ac8b62c/wp_0ac8b62c.html)

Touch is a way we show love, and it is necessary for survival. Our God has created us to receive love and to give love. We were created with this need for love. God Himself is love. He would not create us and then not love us, knowing that love is exactly what we need to live. If we need love, that means we are created to receive and give love. God would go against His nature to make us and then not love us. He is love and He requires us to love as well.

First John 4:16 says, *"And we have known and believed the love that God has for us. God is love, and he who abides in love abides in God, and God in him."* (NKJV) This is the love demonstrated through touch to the infants researched above. God created us to need love, so He loves each one of us. He doesn't just love those who love Him. Remember that Jesus washed Judas' feet too. This all came together for me (Tiffany) several years ago.

When I (Tiffany) had my first child, I received what I know now to be a revelation of the love of God that I have not forgotten. At the time, all I knew was that a light went on in my heart. I understood like never before the love God has for me. My daughter, Kaylee, was four days old, and I took her out in her stroller for a walk around the neighborhood. It was a beautiful spring day, and I love to be outside exercising. The excitement of having this beautiful baby girl in my possession was written all over my face. I was proud, and I was feeling very protective of my child. As I was walking, my thoughts were very much consumed with my new daughter and I was also thanking God for her. Then it hit me - very suddenly. God had a Son, whom He loved even more than I loved Kaylee. And He gave His Son to die for someone like me! I knew that in my head. I had known that for years, but it never hit me until I had a child of my own. And I remember thinking I would never give my daughter to die for anyone, especially not anyone like me or the other sinners in this world. But, God, He loved me so much that He gave His perfect child to die for me. The revelation (understanding) was astounding. It still is.

And this God who loved me enough to give His Son, loves you enough as well. And He loves everyone else that much too. There's nothing God created that He doesn't love. The Scriptures speak about God's love for His creation, especially mankind, over and over again. Understanding the love of God is fundamental to understanding the atonement of Jesus Christ (atonement = Christ's accomplishments on the cross).

God loves everyone the same. Romans 2:11 reads, *"For God does not show favoritism."* Some people believe that God made certain humans for heaven and certain humans for hell. In that argument, God would have to love some people, and not love others. This goes against the very nature of God. For His Word says, *"God is love"* (1 John 4:8).

There are many scriptures that testify to the truth that God loves everyone He created, not just some people. Arguably, the best known scripture in the Bible tells us of God's love for the world. John 3:16 says, *"For God so loved the world_that he gave his one and only Son, that whoever believes in him shall not perish but have eternal life."* Scripture doesn't read, "for God so loved the few. . ." No, it says He loved the "world." That includes all creation. God loves us all and that is the reason for the sacrifice of His Son.

Jesus even teaches that we are not to just love those who love us, but to love even those who do not love us. God will not tell us to do something He will not do Himself.

> *"You have heard that it was said, 'Love your neighbor and hate your enemy.' But I tell you: Love your enemies and pray for those who persecute you, that you may be sons of your Father in heaven.*

He causes his sun to rise on the evil and the good, and sends rain on the righteous and the unrighteous. If you love those who love you, what reward will you get? Are not even the tax collectors doing that? And if you greet only your brothers, what are you doing more than others? Do not even pagans do that? Be perfect, therefore, as your heavenly Father is perfect." (Matthew 5:43-48)

God will do no less than what He tells us to do. He loves perfectly and wills that we love perfectly too. This means we need to love those who love us, and love those who do not love us because God loves those who love Him and He loves those who do not. Love is good, not evil. God is good, not evil.

Love is Jesus Christ. God is love (1 John 4:8b). *"This is how we know what love is: Jesus Christ laid down his life for us. And we ought to lay down our lives for our brothers."* (1John 3:16) That's pure love – the sacrifice of a life. We tend to love conditionally, and only love those who love us. But God is not like us. God loves even those who don't love Him back. He makes the rain fall on the righteous and unrighteous alike.

God even describes what love is. He says,

Love is patient, love is kind. It does not envy, it does not boast, it is not proud. It is not rude, it is not self-seeking, it is not easily angered, it keeps no record of wrongs. Love does not delight in evil but rejoices with the truth. It always protects, always trusts, always hopes, always perseveres. Love never fails.
(1 Corinthians 13:4-8a)

In describing to us what love is, God describes who He is. God is patient, not wanting any to perish (2 Peter 3:9), God is kind, God does not envy. God does not boast, is not proud, is not self-seeking, is not easily angered (thankfully!), and keeps no record of wrongs (*as far as the east is from the west so far has He removed our transgressions from us* – Psalm 103). God does not delight in evil, which would not be true if He created humans just so they would be evil and go to hell. God rejoices with the truth. God always protects (see Psalm 91). God always trusts, always hopes, always perseveres. God never fails!

Second Samuel 14:14 reads, *"Like water spilled on the ground, which cannot be recovered, so we must die. But God does not take away life; instead, he devises ways so that a banished person may not remain estranged from him."* God doesn't desire that we live away from Him, but that we live in communion with Him. He has devised a perfect way so that banished persons may not remain estranged from Him. That perfect way is Jesus Christ.

One of the most interesting stories for children to read is about Jonah and the whale. However, this is not just a children's story. This is a story of God's amazing love and mercy. God reached out to a people not of the Abrahamic covenant. These people were Ninevites, who were Assyrians. They were people who fought the Israelites, yet God called his prophet to go there so He could show them mercy. Jonah didn't agree with God's mercy and ran away. And we know the rest of the story. Eventually, Jonah did go to Ninevah and God spared the people after they repented. It is God's desire to show mercy and offer forgiveness to everyone on Earth who repents, not just a select few. We become prideful when we begin to think we're the only ones Jesus came to save.

God really does not want anyone to perish because He loves us all. *"'I take no pleasure in the death of anyone,' declares the Sovereign LORD. 'Repent and live!'"* (Ezekiel 18:32) When we don't believe this, we make God out to be a liar and the truth is not in us. We need to believe God when He speaks in His Word. He says He doesn't want anyone to perish, and He implores us to repent, believe, and live.

King David writes, *"Your kingdom is an everlasting kingdom, and your dominion endures through all generations. The LORD is faithful to all his* *promises and <u>loving toward all he has made</u>."* (Psalm 145:13) God shows the faithfulness described in this verse through the shedding of the blood of Jesus Christ. He says that He loves **all** that He has made, not just a few people. He loves everyone and everything He has made. He made it all to be good, but as we know, everything became cursed after Adam and Eve chose to sin. However, Jesus brings hope through His blood.

The Lord Jesus Christ took all of the curse upon Himself at the cross, not just some of it. He is LORD of all and every knee will bow to Him, not just some demons, or some knees. His name is greater than any other name, and those who reject this great love are doomed for destruction. Second Peter 2:1 says, *"But there were also false prophets among the people, even as there will be false teachers among you, who will secretly bring in destructive heresies, even denying the Lord who bought them, and bring on themselves swift destruction"* (NKJV). The key words we want to focus on are "who bought them." Jesus bought these people that now deny him. Later in the chapter, after talking about all the evil these people perpetuate, it says, *"For if, after they have escaped the pollutions of the world through the knowledge of the Lord and Savior Jesus Christ, they are again entangled in them and overcome, the latter end is worse for them than the beginning"* (2 Peter 1:20 NKJV). In other words, they are worse off having known Christ and turning away, than if they had never known the Lord. The point here is that Jesus paid for their sins, but they are not saved because they denied Him.

"'Do I take any pleasure in the death of the wicked?' declares the Sovereign LORD. 'Rather, am I not pleased when they turn from their ways and live?'" (Ezekiel 18:23) God is pleased when people turn from evil and choose life, not death. He doesn't want anyone to die without Christ.

It is evident, that just as most parents love their children, the LORD loves His children. Since He is the Creator, all people are His children, so He loves them all. Psalm 27:10 reads, *"Though my father and mother forsake me, the LORD will receive me."* Human love fails, but God's love never does.

CHAPTER 2

The Savior of the World

In the beginning was the Word, and the Word was with God,
and the Word was God. He was with God in the beginning.
Through him all things were made; without him nothing was made that
has been made. In him was life, and that life was the light of men. The
light shines in the darkness, but the darkness has not understood it.
There came a man who was sent from God; his name
was John. He came as a witness to testify concerning that
*light, so that through him **all men might believe.***
(John 1:1-7, author's emphasis)

W hen God created the world, He created man in order to have
fellowship with Him. The Bible tells us that God walked in the
garden of Eden in the cool of the day (Gen 3:8). He enjoyed spending
time with Adam and Eve. It was after Adam and Eve sinned that they
tried to hide themselves from God. The intimate fellowship with God
that Adam and Eve once enjoyed was broken because of disobedience
(sin). This disobedience brought about the curse.

Cursed is the ground because of you; through painful toil you will
eat of it all the days of your life. It will produce thistles for you,

*and you will eat the plants of the field. By the sweat of your brow
you will eat your food until you return to the ground, since from
it you were taken; for dust you are and to dust you will return.*
(Genesis 3:17b-19)

But God doesn't leave it at that. He makes the first sacrifice, using one of
the animals He created. He provides clothing for Adam and Eve out of
animal skins (Gen 3:21). Not only does He make the first sacrifice, but
the last one as well. Jesus Christ is the last and only sacrifice needed for
salvation. God wants all people to be saved and has provided a way for
that to happen. All people sin. We need to be aware of sin in order to be
aware of our need of a Savior.

John the apostle makes God's purpose in Jesus clear in 1 John 4:14
where He states, *"And we have seen and testify that the Father has sent
the Son as Savior of the world."* (NKJV) God's Son was sent to be the
Savior of the world. God says that salvation is *"through faith in Jesus
Christ, to all and on all who believe. For there is no difference; for all have
sinned and fall short of the glory of God, being justified freely by His grace
through the redemption that is in Christ Jesus"* (Romans 3:22-24). This
is atonement.

"Atonement" is the word used to describe what happened on the cross
when Jesus died. Websters Dictionary defines atonement as:

> 1. Amends made for an injury or wrong; EXPIATION. 2. In the
> Hebrew Scriptures man's reconciliation with God after having
> transgressed the covenant. 3. a. the redemptive life and death
> of Christ. b. The reconciliation of God and man thus brought
> about by Christ.

The word atonement is speaking of what Christ accomplished on
the cross. Isaiah prophesied about this event and what Jesus would
accomplish hundreds of years before it happened.

Surely he took up our infirmities and carried our sorrows,
yet we considered him stricken by God,
smitten by him, and afflicted.
But he was pierced for our transgressions,
he was crushed for our iniquities;
the punishment that brought us peace was upon him,
and by his wounds we are healed. Isaiah 53:4-5

This passage answers the question of what Jesus has done. So the question remains, for whom has He done it? Who are the "we" Isaiah is talking about?

The angels at the birth of Jesus proclaimed the "we" when they said, *"Do not be afraid. I bring you good news of great joy that will be for all the people. Today in the town of David a Savior has been born to you; he is Christ the Lord."* (Luke 2:10-11) "All the people" are the "we" Isaiah spoke of so long ago. There is hope for everyone in the world through the blood of Jesus Christ. The Apostle John testifies that Jesus came for the whole world. *"He is the atoning sacrifice for our sins, and not only for ours but also for the sins of the whole world."* (1 John 2:2) The whole world means everyone.

Jesus is the Savior of the world, if the world will believe. The arguably best known scripture in the Bible tells us clearly that God loves the world and Jesus came for the world. John 3:16 reads, *"For God so loved the world that he gave his one and only Son, that whoever believes in him shall not perish but have eternal life."* First John 4:14 reads, *"And we have seen and testify that the Father has sent the Son as Savior of the world." (NKJV)* Jesus is Savior of the world, if we believe, and not just believe mentally. For *"even the demons believe - and tremble"* (James 2:19 NKJV).

Even John the Baptist testified that Jesus came to save the world. John 1:29 says, *"The next day John saw Jesus coming toward him and said, 'Look, the Lamb of God, who takes away the sin of the world.'"* John the

9

Baptist prophesied about Jesus, telling his hearers what Jesus would accomplish at Calvary.

Later, after rising from the dead, Jesus gave us a job to do in accordance with what He had already done. He came to save the world, and we are to go out and tell the world the good news. Salvation is through Christ alone. *"He said to them, 'Go into <u>all the world</u> and preach the good news to <u>all creation</u>. Whoever believes and is baptized will be saved, but whoever does not believe will be condemned.'"* (Mark 16:15) This is commonly labeled the Great Commission. It tells us to go into "all" the world, preaching to "all" creation. This would be meaningless and a waste of time if not everyone had equal opportunity to be saved. Our God is not a time-waster. He wouldn't tell us to do this, unless He wanted the world to be saved. So, take heart – He's after you! This Truth is evident in one of Paul's letters: *". . . that God was <u>reconciling the world to himself in Christ</u>, not counting men's sins against them."* (2 Corinthians 5:19) God reconciled the "world" to himself through Christ, not just a few people.

These passages make it obvious that Jesus came to save all the world, not just a few "chosen." We are only chosen because we believe. First Timothy 4:9-10 says it well. *"This is a trustworthy saying that deserves full acceptance (and for this we strive), that we have put our hope in the <u>living God, who is the savior of all men, and especially of those who believe.</u>"* Read that last part with us again. Christ is the "savior of all men, and especially of those who believe." Christ came for the world, but only those who believe are saved. Romans 1:16 says, *"I am not ashamed of the gospel because it is the power of God for the salvation of everyone who believes: first for the Jew, then for the Gentile."* Everyone who believes is saved.

Paul wrote about a body of Jews who kept the disciples from speaking to the Gentiles. He writes that the Judeans, *"killed both the Lord Jesus and their own prophets, and have persecuted us; and they do not please*

God and are contrary to all men, forbidding us to speak to the Gentiles that they may be saved . . ." (1 Thessalonians 2:15-16 NKJV). It is obvious from this passage that God desired the Gentiles to be saved, or He wouldn't send Paul to them in order to preach. It is also evident that there is a battle in the heavenly realms going on to keep people from being saved, as evidenced from the Judeans forbidding the disciples to preach.

Many more passages speak of the "we" as well. A few are listed below. Read these. Meditate on the implication of what they are saying. It brings new urgency to the Great Commission to make disciples of all nations, baptizing them in the name of the Father, the Son, and the Spirit.

- *For there is one God and mediator between God and men, the man Christ Jesus, who gave himself as a ransom for all men – the testimony given in its proper time.* (1 Tim 2:5-6)

- *Here is a trustworthy saying that deserves full acceptance: Christ Jesus came into the world to save sinners—of whom I am the worst.* (1 Timothy 1:15)
  We know that everybody is a sinner. Well, that's who Christ came to save! Everybody is included in this.

- *"Turn to me and be saved, all you ends of the earth; for I am God, and there is no other."* (Isaiah 45:22)

- *"This is good, and pleases God our Savior, who wants all men to be saved and to come to a knowledge of the truth."* (1 Timothy 2:3-4)

- *"In the same way your Father in heaven is not willing that any of these little ones should be lost."* (Matthew 18:14)
  God is not "willing" that anyone be lost! What hope we have!

- *"For the Son of Man did not come to destroy men's lives but to save them."* (Luke 9:56)

  The mission of Jesus Christ was to save mankind.

- *In putting everything under him, God left nothing that is not subject to him. Yet at present we do not see everything subject to him. But we see Jesus, who was made a little lower than the angels, now crowned with glory and honor because he suffered death, so that by the grace of God <u>he might taste death for everyone.</u>* (Hebrews 2: 8-9)

  Because of what Jesus has done, no one needs to go to hell. Obviously some do because they do not believe in the Son of God, but Christ has tasted death for "everyone."

Not only is the LORD the Savior of the world, but He is patient because He wants everyone to repent and be saved, not just a few. Second Peter 3:9 says, *"The Lord is not slack concerning His promise, as some count slackness, but is longsuffering toward us, not willing that any should perish but that all should come to repentance."* (NKJV) God wants **all** people to repent and be saved. "All" includes everyone. Another version of the same verse reads, *"He is patient with you, <u>not wanting anyone to perish, but everyone to come to repentance."</u>* (NIV)

God couldn't want something He didn't provide for. If God wants you to do something, He's going to provide for it. If God wants something done, He's going to provide for it. So, if the Word says that God wants everyone to be saved, then He has provided for that salvation. He doesn't want anyone to perish, which means He wants everyone to be saved. We know that not everyone is saved, but that is not because the LORD didn't provide a way for them to be saved. That is because they chose to deny Christ, which we'll discuss in a later chapter.

We need to understand that God is not a liar and if He tells us to do something, He'll provide a way for that. A more detailed "Great

Commission" is given in Mark 16:15-18. This is what Jesus says is our job description as believers:

> *Go into all the world and preach the good news to all creation. Whoever believes and is baptized will be saved, but whoever does not believe will be condemned. And these signs will accompany those who believe: In my name they will drive out demons; they will speak in new tongues; they will pick up snakes with their hands; and when they drink deadly poison, it will not hurt them at all; they will place their hands on sick people, and they will recover.*

If God is telling us to do the above feats in the name of Christ, that means that Christ has to have broken the power of the enemy through the atonement. God doesn't say, "Just drive out the demons that are on certain people because Jesus doesn't have authority over the others." No! He tells us that all things are under the feet of Jesus Christ and we are seated with Him in the heavenly realms in a place of authority (Ephesians 1 & 2). The atonement covers it all. Jesus is Lord of all! It's the job of the believer to spread the Kingdom of God on earth through the grace that God gives us for empowerment.

God doesn't desire us to be lost, but to be saved. Christ didn't leave anyone out when He died on the cross, but we leave ourselves out when we don't believe the Truth. This atonement of Christ covers **all** creation.

Titus 2:11 says, *"For the grace of God that brings salvation has appeared to all men."* This is the Hope of the world. This is Jesus.

CHAPTER 3

Freewill

Even though the Lord purchased us with His blood, He will not force anyone to be His bondservant. In Scripture, a bondservant was one who was able to go free, but loved his master so much that he chose to be his slave for the rest of his life. We, too, are free to choose whether we will be bondservants or not. God allows us to choose whether we will serve Him or not, because freedom is required for true worship or true obedience from the heart. There can be no obedience from the heart unless there is the freedom to disobey. (Rick Joyner, *Overcoming Fear*, p.47)

We have freewill. Just because God is sovereign, doesn't mean that He makes our choices for us. The Word says we have to believe in Jesus and confess Him as LORD in order to be saved. It does NOT say that either we're saved or we're not and we have no say in it.

John 8:24 reads, *"Therefore I said to you that you will die in your sins; for if you do not believe that I am He, you will die in your sins"* (NKJV). Our beliefs, or our faith, will determine whether we die in our sins, or live in victory.

Jesus is the way the Truth and the Life. No one comes to the Father except through Him. Believe on the LORD Jesus Christ and you shall be saved. You have to choose. The choice isn't made for you. John 14:6 says, *"Jesus answered, 'I am the way and the truth and the life. No one comes to the Father except through me.'"*

We learned in Chapter One that God loves us all and we learned in Chapter Two that Jesus came to set everyone free. However, it is only those who choose to receive the freedom offered that are saved. It is God's will to save everyone. However, as we read in Luke, some are not willing to be saved. Luke 7:30 reads, *"But the Pharisees and lawyers rejected the will of God for themselves . . ."* (NKJV). It was God's will that the Pharisees and lawyers be saved, but they refused that salvation.

King David writes *"Salvation is far from the wicked, for they do not seek out your decrees"* (Psalm 119:155). Why is salvation far from the wicked? It is because they do not seek God. Is it then impossible for them to be saved? No, not at all. However, they need to seek God and He promises to be found by them.

Additionally, there needs to be an understanding of sin and repentance. People need to know that the only reason they need a Savior is because they choose to sin. We all choose to sin; therefore, we all stand condemned without the blood of Jesus. There's an interesting paragraph written by A.W. Tozer that speaks to man's desire to sin.

> [A] doctrinal hindrance is the teaching that men are so weak by nature that they are unable to keep the law of God. Our moral helplessness is hammered into us in sermon and song until we wilt under it and give up in despair. And on top of this we are told that we must accept Jesus in order that we may be saved from the wrath of the broken law! No matter what the intellect may say, the human heart can never accept the idea that we are to be held responsible for breaking a law that we cannot keep.

Would a father lay upon the back of his three-year-old son a sack of grain weighing five-hundred pounds and then beat the child because he could not carry it? Either men can or they cannot please God. If they cannot, they are not morally responsible, and have nothing to fear. If they *can*, and *will not*, then they are guilty, and as guilty sinners they will be sent to hell at last. The latter is undoubtedly the fact. If the Bible is allowed to speak for itself it will teach loudly the doctrine of man's personal responsibility for sins committed. Men sin because they want to sin. God's quarrel with men is that they will not do even that part of the will of God which they understand and could do if they would.
(*Paths to Power* p. 45)

We are responsible for our sins. Until the desires of our hearts line up completely with the desires of God's heart, we will keep on sinning. However, Jesus in His mercy and love came to pay the price for that sin so that we may be saved. We are able to choose to sin and we are able to choose salvation.

There's an interesting quote from Rick Joyner in the small booklet titled *Overcoming Witchcraft*. He states:

The Battle of Armageddon is fought in the **"valley of Decision" (see Joel 3:14);** everyone on earth will be brought to the place of making a decision. It is a power confrontation, and the choice is being made concerning issues of power and authority. We will choose either the power and authority of God or the power and authority of the evil one – but we will choose. (p. 49-50)

The choice is ours. God didn't make a bunch of robots, but he made people that He loves in His own image with freewill.

There's a story Jesus tells in which the master directs a faithful and wise manager to be in charge of his servants. The warning is that if the manager does not treat the servants right, he will be cast out. Jesus says the master will come at a day and time the manager does not expect him and *"He will cut him [the manager] to pieces and assign him a place with the unbelievers"* (Luke 12:46). The manager has a choice here. He is one of the servants, but can quickly fall and be no better than an unbeliever if he is not doing that which the master tells him to do when the master returns. The implications here are great for a believer in Jesus Christ. We are shown there is a choice. We believe or we don't. However, the belief indicates an action. James says, *"But someone will say, 'You have faith; I have deeds.' Show me your faith without deeds, and I will show you my faith by what I do"* (James 2:18). Faith and deeds work together here. If we have faith in Jesus, we are saved; but we need to believe. The choice is not made for us.

Our choice can even be hindered by what others teach us. Jesus rebukes the Pharisees, saying, *"Woe to you, teachers of the law and Pharisees, you hypocrites! You shut the kingdom of heaven in men's faces. You yourselves do not enter, nor will you let those enter who are trying to."* (Matthew 23:13-14) These people are trying to be saved. They want to believe, but the teachers and Pharisees put such a yoke on them, that they cannot. They obscure the way for those who want to enter in. It's a battle. We have a very real enemy that we have to fight in the spiritual realm. The teachers and Pharisees are very dedicated. They work hard and go far and wide to convert a person, but the person doesn't end up saved because they twist the message and add rules taught by men. *"Woe to you, teachers of the law and Pharisees, you hypocrites! You travel over land and sea to win a single convert, and when he becomes one, you make him twice as much a son of hell as you are."* (Matthew 23:15) Some teachers make it so difficult to be saved by adding their own rules, that people are deceived into thinking they're saved, when they're not.

On the other hand, some people just don't want to be saved. They'd rather stay the way they are, afraid of what they might lose if they give their lives to Jesus. Christ laments this, saying, *"O Jerusalem, Jerusalem, you who kill the prophets and stone those sent to you, how often I have longed to gather your children together, as a hen gathers her chicks under her wings, but you were not willing."* (Matthew 23:37) Jesus shows the unwillingness of people to be saved. This is contrasted with God's own longing and willingness to save them.

Jesus tells a parable that illustrates this:

> *A certain man was preparing a great banquet and invited many guests. At the time of the banquet he sent his servant to tell those who had been invited, "Come, for everything is now ready."*
> *But they all alike began to make excuses. The first said, "I have just bought a field, and I must go and see it. Please excuse me."*
> *Another said, "I have just bought five yoke of oxen, and I am on my way to try them out. Please excuse me."*
> *Still another said, "I just got married, so I can't come."*
> *The servant came back and reported this to his master. Then the owner of the house became angry and ordered his servant, "Go out quickly into the streets and alleys of the town and bring in the poor, the crippled, the blind and the lame."*
> *"Sir," the servant said, "what you ordered has been done, but there is still room."*
> *Then the master told his servant, "Go out to the roads and country lanes and make them come in, so that my house will be full. I tell you, not one of those men who were invited will get a taste of my banquet."* Luke 14:16-24

These people that were invited refused to come. They were definitely invited, as we all are. However, they refused, as people sometimes do. The Lord did not make their choice for them, but the people chose lesser things over participating in the "feast in the kingdom of God" (v. 15). People refuse God. God doesn't refuse them, but invites them all. *"They perish because <u>they refused</u> to love the truth and so be saved."* (2 Thessalonians 2:10b, TNIV) The message of the gospel is clear.

"Whoever believes and is baptized will be saved, but whoever does not believe will be condemned." (Mark 16:16) We have to believe.

Acts 13:38-41 reads,

Therefore, my brothers, I want you to know that through Jesus the forgiveness of sins is proclaimed to you. Through him everyone who believes is justified from everything you could not be justified from by the law of Moses. Take care that what the prophets have said does not happen to you: "Look, you scoffers, wonder and perish, for I am going to do something in your days that you would never believe, even if someone told you."

God is adamant that everyone who believes is justified through the blood of Jesus. Those who believe are saved. We are admonished to take care that we do not become scoffers and that we do believe even if no one tells us to believe. Faith is the "substance of things not seen." We are to believe even if we don't see anything that remotely looks like what God promises in His Word. His is a marvelous salvation and we must believe it.

Even though God provides such a marvelous way of salvation, He is not going to make anyone choose life. Luke writes, *"But some of them became obstinate; they refused to believe and publicly maligned the Way. So Paul left them . . ."* (Acts 19:9). These people refused to believe. They could have had eternal life with Christ, but refused to do so. It's like when a parent puts a child to bed. They can give the child a warm bed in a safe home, turn the lights out and give him a teddy bear to sleep with. However, the parent cannot make the child sleep. Everything is provided for the child to sleep, but the child is stubbornly able to refuse if he so chooses. Obviously, this is not a direct parallel to salvation, but it gives you an idea of what we're talking about.

The book of Acts is full of stories of people who chose life and those who refused to believe and in that refusal, chose death. Acts 14:2 says, *"But the Jews who refused to believe stirred up the Gentiles and poisoned their minds against the brothers."* The Word says that these Jews "refused" to believe. It doesn't say they couldn't believe, but that they refused to. They obviously had a choice here and they chose unwisely. This is contrasted with people who do believe later on. *"They preached the good news in that city and won a large number of disciples."* (Acts 14:21a) The word "won" indicates a battle; whereas, no battle is needed if everything is predetermined and man has nothing to do with it.

It is through the gospel (good news) of Jesus Christ that we are saved, not some predetermined thought of God. *"By this gospel you are saved, if you hold firmly to the word I preached to you. Otherwise, you have believed in vain."* (1 Corinthians 15:2) *"Salvation is found in no one else, for there is no other name under heaven given to men by which we must be saved."* (Acts 4:12) This is a great salvation, as the writer of Hebrews testifies:

> *We must pay more careful attention, therefore, to what we have heard, so that we do not drift away. For if the message spoken by angels was binding, and every violation and disobedience received its just punishment, how shall we escape if we ignore such a great salvation? This salvation, which was first announced by the Lord, was confirmed to us by those who heard him. God also testified to it by signs, wonders and various miracles, and gifts of the Holy Spirit distributed according to his will.*
> (Hebrews 2:1-4)

We can ignore, or disbelieve the message and so be lost. Unbelief is a hindrance to salvation because it is the opposite of faith. The writer of Hebrews begs us to not harden our hearts. Hebrews 3:19 sums it up: *"So we see that they were not able to enter, because of their unbelief."*

> *For the Scripture says, "Whoever believes on Him will not be put to shame." For there is no distinction between Jew and Greek, for the same Lord over all is rich to all who call upon Him. For "whoever calls on the name of the LORD shall be saved."* (Romans 10:11-13)

Whoever calls on Jesus is saved. The whole Bible testifies to this. *"To Him [Jesus] all the prophets witness that, through His name, whoever believes in Him will receive remission of sins."* (Acts 10:43) All the prophets testify that we must believe.

Jesus tells an interesting parable in the gospels. In it, He describes the Word of God as seed scattered about and the response of those upon whom it falls.

> *A farmer went out to sow his seed. As he was scattering the seed, some fell along the path; it was trampled on, and the birds of the air ate it up. Some fell on rock, and when it came up, the plants withered because they had no moisture. Other seed fell among thorns, which grew up with it and choked the plants. Still other seed fell on good soil. It came up and yielded a crop, a hundred times more than was sown.* (Luke 8:5-8a)

Then Jesus goes on to explain what the parable means:

> *This is the meaning of the parable: The seed is the word of God. Those along the path are the ones who hear, and then the devil comes and takes away the word from their hearts, so that they may not believe and be saved. Those on the rock are the ones who received the word with joy when they heard it, but they have no root. They believe for a while, but in the time of testing they fall away. The seed that fell among the thorns stands for those who hear, but as they go on their way they are choked by life's worries, riches and pleasures, and they do not mature. But the seed on good soil stands for those with a noble and good heart, who hear the word, retain it, and by persevering produce a crop.* (Luke 8:11-15)

The seed is scattered on all places (all people), but Jesus describes the results, not in terms of the hearers being able or being unable to believe because God predestined them for hell, but because the devil steals it (one of his job descriptions); those who don't appreciate testing, and decide it's too difficult to be a Christian; those who believe lies of worry, etc.; and finally, those who receive the word and persevere in it, not only being saved, but saving others.

Jesus goes on to admonish us a few verses later (v. 18) to be obedient to the voice of God. *"Therefore consider carefully how you listen."* If it was not up to us at least to some degree, we would not be admonished to listen and obey for it really wouldn't matter whether we listened and obeyed or not. However, if you choose Jesus as Savior and Lord, you are *"not of those who shrink back and are destroyed, but of those <u>who believe and are saved</u>"* (Hebrews 10:39).

Those who are saved are those who believe. *"For since, in the wisdom of God, the world through wisdom did not know God, it pleased God through the foolishness of the message preached to <u>save those who believe</u>"* (1 Cor 1:21 NKJV). John 3:34 reiterates this. *"<u>He who believes</u> in the Son has everlasting life; and he who does not believe the Son shall not see life, but the wrath of God abides on him"*.

We do not need to be afraid of the wrath of God if we choose what is right – the first step is declaring Jesus Christ as Lord and Savior. *"<u>If</u> you do what is right, will you not be accepted? But <u>if</u> you do not do what is right, sin is crouching at your door; it desires to have you, but you must rule over it"* (Genesis 4:7 TNIV, authors' emphasis). This passage indicates a choice. The LORD Himself was speaking here and telling Cain that he must make a choice and rule over sin. If not, the sin crouching at his door would rule him.

Some other scriptures to read and meditate on regarding choosing life and holiness are below. Please read these and ask the Holy Spirit to give you revelation (understanding) into them.

- *[Jesus became the] source of eternal life for all who obey Him.* (Hebrews 5:9)
  Obedience is optional; we can quench the Holy Spirit.

- *Make every effort . . . to be holy; without holiness no one will see the LORD.* (Hebrews 12:14)
  Being holy takes our effort through grace, which is empowerment.

- *Whoever turns a sinner from the error of his way will save him from death and cover over a multitude of sins.* (James 5:20)
  Our effort again through grace, which is the empowerment of God to do good and resist evil.

- *But just as he who called you is holy, so be holy in all you do; for it is written: "Be holy, because I am holy."* (1 Peter 1:15-16)

So, if there was no freewill, and we were created to either perish in hell or live in heaven, what would happen if a person chosen for heaven did not obey God? Why would it be "hard for the righteous to be saved," as scripture indicates if God had already decided before a person ever even lived whether or not they were destined for hell or heaven? Answer: We must decide to follow the gospel of God. Otherwise, this makes no sense.

But in keeping with His promise we are looking forward to a new heaven and a new earth, where righteousness dwells. So then, dear friends, since you are looking forward to this, make every effort to be found spotless, blameless and at peace with Him. Bear in mind that our Lord's patience means salvation, just as our dear brother Paul also wrote you with the wisdom that God gave him. He writes the same way in all his letters, speaking in them of these matters. His letters contain some things that are hard to understand, which ignorant and unstable people distort, as they do the other Scriptures, to their own destruction. 2 Peter 3:13-16 (TNIV)

"Make every effort"? Sounds like a choice, doesn't it? "Our Lord's patience means salvation"? Why would God need to be patient with us if we did not have an ability to choose life or death? If there was no ability to choose life or death, why would God say we need to choose life or death? Scripture only makes sense if people have freedom to choose Christ or reject Him. If the choice is made for us, there is no freedom.

"For God so loved the world that he gave his one and only Son, that <u>whoever believes in him shall not perish but have eternal life</u>" (John 3:16). We have to decide to believe or not.

> *Whoever believes in the Son of God accepts this testimony. Whoever does not believe God has made him out to be a liar, because they have not believed the testimony God has given about his Son. And this is the testimony: God has given us eternal life, and this life is in his Son. Whoever has the Son has life; whoever does not have the Son of God does not have life.* (1 John 5:10-12 TNIV)

We are told we can choose to accept "His testimony." But if we choose not to believe, we "make Him out to be a liar." Again, this is dependant on our choice.

Some may say, but what about predestination? We are definitely predestined in the sense that the Lord knows everything. He knows the choice we will make, but He still allows us to make it. Romans 8:29a says, *"Those God foreknew, He also predestined. . ."* Foreknew means "knew beforehand." God knows ahead of time who will choose life and who will choose death. It doesn't mean that He chooses for us.

We are also told to *"Fight the good fight of the faith. Take hold of the eternal life to which you were called when you made your good confession"* (1 Tim 6:12). We were called to eternal life after we made our "good confession." This confession of Christ requires faith. The Word says, *"Therefore, since we have been justified through faith, we have peace with God through our Lord Jesus Christ, through whom we have gained access by faith into this grace in which we now stand. And we rejoice in the hope of the glory of God"* (Romans 5:1-2).

The justification we receive when we believe turns us from sinners into saints. Paul writes to the Corinthians, *"To the church of God which is at Corinth, to those who are sanctified in Christ Jesus, called to be saints, with all who in every place call on the name of Jesus Christ our Lord, both theirs and ours"* (1 Corinthians 1:2 NKJV). Those who call on Jesus are called to be saints and are sanctified in Christ Jesus.

Not all people God creates are justified or sanctified, but it is not because He doesn't desire it for them. Jesus says,

> For I have come down from heaven not to do my will but to do the will of him who sent me, that I shall lose none of all that he has given me, but raise them up at the last day. For my Father's will is that everyone who looks to the Son and believes in him shall have eternal life, and I will raise him up at the last day. (John 6:38-40)

Jesus clearly describes the will of God here. God's will is that **everyone** who looks to Jesus for salvation and believes is saved.

We are told the way is narrow and only a few find it – meaning it's a tough path to give your life fully and completely to Jesus Christ.

> Enter through the narrow gate. For wide is the gate and broad is the road that leads to destruction, and many enter through it.

But small is the gate and narrow the road that leads to life, and only a few find it. (Matthew 7:13-14)

Jesus is telling us to enter through the narrow gate (Himself) to be saved. He tells us that we have a choice regarding which gate we will enter. If we didn't have a choice, there would be no need for this statement.

> *This is the message we have heard from him and declare to you: God is light; in him there is no darkness at all. If we claim to have fellowship with him and yet walk in the darkness, we lie and do not live out the truth. But if we walk in the light, as he is in the light, we have fellowship with one another, and the blood of Jesus, his Son, purifies us from all sin. If we claim to be without sin, we deceive ourselves and the truth is not in us. If we confess our sins, he is faithful and just and will forgive us our sins and purify us from all unrighteousness. If we claim we have not sinned, we make him out to be a liar and his word is not in us.* 1 John 1:5-10 (TNIV)

The blood of Jesus is the "spiritual soap" in verse nine that purifies us from "all unrighteousness." Does this blood purify every person? No. We need to apply the blood of Jesus through faith. We need to walk in the light; we need to choose to confess our sins. Verse seven says, "If we walk in the light . . ." The word "if" means we have to decide what we will do. The passage also says, "If we confess our sins. . ." God doesn't cause, make, or predestine us to confess our sins, we must choose to. He will certainly convict us of our sins because He disciplines those He loves and does not want us to sin. However, we have to choose to repent of those sins in order to be free.

> *For it is time for judgment to begin with God's household; and if it begins with us, what will the outcome be for those who do not obey the gospel of God? And,*
> *"If it is hard for the righteous to be saved, what will become of the ungodly and the sinner?"*
> 1 Peter 4:17-18 (TNIV)

It is infinitely easier to keep on sinning and not confess Jesus as Lord and really mean it – really have it change your life. However, the narrow path is not the easy path, which is why only a few find it.

This is why Jude exhorts his readers to "contend for the faith" and keep on the narrow path.

> *Dear friends, although I was very eager to write to you about the salvation we share, I felt I had to write and urge you to contend for the faith that was once for all entrusted to the saints. For certain men whose condemnation was written about long ago have secretly slipped in among you. They are godless men, who change the grace of our God into a license for immorality and deny Jesus Christ our only Sovereign and Lord. Though you already know all this, I want to remind you that the Lord delivered his people out of Egypt, but later destroyed those who did not believe. And the angels who did not keep their positions of authority but abandoned their own home—these he has kept in darkness, bound with everlasting chains for judgment on the great Day. In a similar way, Sodom and Gomorrah and the surrounding towns gave themselves up to sexual immorality and perversion. They serve as an example of those who suffer the punishment of eternal fire.* (Jude 1:3-7)

In verse three, "contend for the faith" means "to strive or vie in contest or rivalry or against difficulties: struggle." Why would we have to do that if God had predetermined who would go to heaven and who would go to hell? Our fate would be fixed, as well as everyone else's. No, it means just what it says. We struggle against our enemy for our faith. Although God is in control, He lets Satan have enough leeway to do his job (kill, steal, destroy, lie). God allows us to accept the gift of grace or reject it.

What is meant by faith here? Does it mean enough "faith" so that we're obedient to Christ in the great commission? (We must remember that the great commission wasn't the only command of Christ.) We're supposed to heal the sick, raise the dead, and cast out demons too. Love is supposed to be the motivator, not obedience out of some kind of legalistic, Pharisaical duty.

A lot of the Old Testament prophecy is a type and shadow of being saved through Jesus Christ. So, Egypt in verse five represents the world and hell, and the promised land represents Godliness and heaven. The Israelites who did not believe God were destroyed (they never reached the promised land) because they were disobedient and stiff-necked. They turned from God (chose disobedience). They certainly believed in God, but even the demons do that. The unbelief of the first generation of Israelites kept them out of the promised land.

Likewise, the angels were not created to (or made to) give up their positions; they abandoned them (chose to leave their positions). Verse seven speaks of the similarities between this and the way Sodom and Gomorrah "gave themselves up" (chose) to go the way of immorality and perversion. They "serve as an example" of those who suffer the punishment of eternal fire.

Angels that gave up their positions, however, will not be saved. Jesus came to save humans only. The writer of Hebrews explains who Jesus came to save.

> *Inasmuch then as the children have partaken of flesh and blood, He Himself likewise shared in the same, that through death He might destroy him who had the power of death, that is, the devil, and release those who through fear of death were all their lifetime subject to bondage. For indeed He does not give aid to angels, but He does give aid to the seed of Abraham.* (Hebrews 2:14-16, NKJV)

God also tells us in Hebrews that we will not escape if we "neglect so great a salvation" (Heb 2:3 NKJV). The very idea of being able to neglect something means we have a choice in whether or not we will accept it. It is important to remember that Jesus is not a thief that would steal your heart and life. He will not take your life to be His in eternity by force. He wants you to choose Him. He desires a relationship with you. He longs for you to turn to Him for salvation. The devil's job description is to steal, kill, and destroy. But, Jesus came so that we may have life and have it abundantly.

Additionally, Romans 1:16 says, "*I am not ashamed of the gospel, because it is the power of God for the salvation of everyone who believes: first for the Jew, then for the Gentile.*" This is salvation for all who believe.

Belief takes faith and faith helps us to overcome to the saving of our souls. A theme in the letters to the churches in the book of Revelation is the need to overcome. Jesus tells every church that they need to overcome. This would be completely unnecessary if people were predestined in the sense that the choice of salvation was made for them. It shows our need to push into the Holy of Holies and trust Jesus to keep us in the Kingdom. It takes faith and perseverance, not a false theology that tells us we're saved when we're really not. For then we may become like the church in Laodicea that Jesus says He will "spit" out of His mouth because they try to be a part of the world and a part of the Kingdom. We cannot have both. (Read Revelation chapters two and three for further study.)

CHAPTER 4

God of Hope

Hope deferred makes the heart sick, but a longing fulfilled is a tree of life.
Proverbs 13:12

"Hope Now", a song by Addison Road says, "Everything rides on hope now. Everything rides on faith somehow."

We agree. Where there is no hope, there is no life and there can be no faith. Webster's Dictionary defines hope as: *To wish for something with expectation of its fulfillment; to have confidence; TRUST; to expect and desire.* This is a far cry from the worldly hope all around us that says, "Well maybe it will happen and maybe it won't, but I sure hope it does." No, Godly hope is a confident expectation.

Our God is a God of hope. He tells us that hope is one of the three great things we need to possess (the other two being faith and love). Without hope, people go into depression, despair, and even die. God says that He gives life and gives it abundantly. That's hope. Many passages of scripture speak of hope. Psalm 42:5 (AMP) says, *"Why are you cast down, O my inner self? And why should you moan over me and be disquieted within me? Hope in God and wait expectantly for Him, for I shall yet praise Him, my Help and my God."* The Psalmist speaks hope to himself when he is discouraged and feeling down. He knows that God will come through. He remembers that God's reputation is one of keeping His promises. *"And now, Lord, what do I wait for and expect? My hope and expectation are in You"* (Psalm 39:7 AMP).

We can only really have hope if what we are hoping in has a reputation of reliability. Our God is very reliable. He is faithful to all His promises. *"Behold, the Lord's eye is upon those who fear Him [who revere and worship Him with awe], who wait for Him and hope in His mercy and loving-kindness"* (Psalm 33:18 AMP). God knows those who believe His promises. He knows when we are hoping in Him. He is faithful. He is worthy of our hope.

Our lives are filled with hope, whether we realize it or not. However, you can have no hope if you cannot choose life. It's those people who believe there is no way out that give up on life. We have to believe there is hope of salvation for all mankind, or else that would mean there are people out there without any hope. That totally contradicts who God says He is and what His Word says about Him.

There is no point to the great commission without the hope of salvation. We are told to go out into "all the world." That means the world has hope because of Jesus Christ. Jesus speaks a message of hope in the following passage.

> *Then one said to Him, "Lord, are there few who are saved?" And He said to them, "Strive to enter through the narrow gate, for many, I say to you, will seek to enter and will not be able. When once the Master of the house has risen up and shut the door, and you begin to stand outside and knock at the door, saying, 'Lord, Lord, open for us,' and He will answer and say to you, I do not know you, where you are from, . .'"* (Luke 13:23-25)

In response to the man's question, Jesus tells us to strive to enter through the narrow gate. If Jesus tells us to try to be saved, then there's hope. Our God is a God of salvation, and where there is salvation, there is hope.

We have hope in knowing that God made us and knows us. Paul speaks of this hope to the Athenians in Acts 17.

> *The God who made the world and everything in it is the Lord of heaven and earth and does not live in temples built by human hands. And he is not served by human hands, as if he needed anything, because he himself gives all men life and breath and everything else. From one man he made every nation of men, that they should inhabit the whole earth; and he determined the times set for them and the exact places where they should live. God did this so that men would seek him and perhaps reach out for him and find him, though he is not far from each one of us. "For in him we live and move and have our being." As some of your own poets have said, "We are his offspring." (Acts 17:24-28)*

Paul shows the Athenians that God wants people to seek Him and find Him. It is His desire, and it should give us hope.

Paul continues to portray this hope of salvation for all who believe when he says in 1 Corinthians 9:22, *"I have become all things to all men so that by all possible means I might save some."* Paul would not need to go to this extreme if there was a limited atonement that only saved some and was not offered to all people.

In Noah's day, the LORD told Noah to build a humungous ark. Whoever and whatever entered the ark would be saved from the flooding rains. The whole time Noah and his sons built this ark, Noah preached a message of repentance to the people of the earth (2 Pet 2:5). It's possible that people came from all over the earth in order to see the crazy preacher of righteousness building a boat on dry land. Noah probably looked like a fool to those around him. But, there was hope for those who would enter the ark. And in the end, God wiped out those who were not righteous. They had a choice, and they chose evil over good.

God also calls us "ambassadors for Christ." Second Corinthians 5:20 (NKJV) reads, *"Now then, we are ambassadors for Christ, as though God were pleading through us: we implore you on Christ's behalf, be reconciled to God."* God pleads for reconciliation. There's great hope in this statement because it shows how much God desires all people to be saved.

There's hope even for those who are not preached to, who don't see signs and wonders, or who don't have access to a Bible. Romans 1:20 says,

> *For since the creation of the world God's invisible qualities – his eternal power and divine nature – have been clearly seen, being understood from what has been made, so that men are without excuse.*

Even looking at nature – whatever God has created – shows the glory of God, so that we are without excuse. It's obvious there is a God, and since it's obvious, we ought to search Him out. He says that if we seek Him with all our hearts, we'll find him.

- *But if from there you seek the LORD your God, you will find him if you look for him with all your heart and with all your soul.* (Deuteronomy 4:29)

- *You will seek me and find me when you seek me with all your heart.* (Jeremiah 29:13)

- *"Ask and it will be given to you; seek and you will find; knock and the door will be opened to you. For everyone who asks receives; he who seeks finds; and to him who knocks, the door will be opened."* (Matthew 7:7)

- *"So I say to you: Ask and it will be given to you; seek and you will find; knock and the door will be opened to you. For everyone who asks receives; he who seeks finds; and to him who knocks, the door will be opened."* (Luke 11:9)

Again, this is a message of hope. If the LORD says to seek Him, it's because He wants to be found. He stands at the door and knocks. We just have to let Him in and then we will have fellowship with Him. (Rev. 3:20)

Receive this message of hope. It is held out to you this day. Receive it and then turn around and hold out that same message of hope in Jesus Christ to someone else.

Now may the God of hope fill you with all joy and peace in believing, that you may abound in hope by the power of the Holy Spirit. (Romans 15:13, NKJV)

CHAPTER 5

What Does It Mean to Be God's Elect?

Proverbs 1:24-33 (New Living Translation)

24 "I called you so often, but you wouldn't come.
   I reached out to you, but you paid no attention.

25 You ignored my advice
   and rejected the correction I offered.

26 So I will laugh when you are in trouble!
   I will mock you when disaster overtakes you—

27 when calamity overtakes you like a storm,
   when disaster engulfs you like a cyclone,
   and anguish and distress overwhelm you.

28 "When they cry for help, I will not answer.
   Though they anxiously search for me, they will not find
   me.

29 For **they hated knowledge**
   and **chose not** to fear the LORD.

30 **They rejected** my advice
   and paid no attention when I corrected them.

31 **Therefore, they must eat the bitter fruit of living their
   own way,**
   choking on their own schemes.

³² For simpletons turn away from me—to death.

Fools are destroyed by their own complacency.

³³ **But all who listen to me will live in peace,**
untroubled by fear of harm."

God created man and woman with freewill. We have been allowed to make choices to our good or detriment since the beginning. God put the Tree of the Knowledge of Good and Evil in the garden because we needed to have a choice to obey or not to obey. Without freedom to obey or disobey, there can be no real love. This choice given to Adam and Eve was a choice between life and death. They ended up choosing death. This same choice between life and death is highlighted throughout the Bible. In fact, we make choices between life and death each day. God says that the wages of sin is death. So, if we sin, we're really choosing death. The only thing that saves us from our choices is Jesus Christ. Joshua sets an example for us all to follow when he says, *"Choose this day whom you will serve . . . but as for me and my household, we will serve the Lord"* (Joshua 24:15). It's the same choice Moses set before the Israelites when he said, *"See, I set before you life and prosperity, death and destruction"* (Deuteronomy 30:15). The Israelites are told to choose and we are told to choose as well. We have freedom to choose. As Dr. Dobson puts it, " . . . love demands freedom" (*The Strong-Willed Child, p. 221).*

When you choose Christ, you become one of God's elect. John 1:12-13 reads, *"Yet to all who received him, to those who believed in his name, he gave the right to become children of God – children born not of natural descent, nor of human decision or a husband's will, but born of God."* This is the good news! Paul writes of this election in his letter to the Romans. When we believe in Jesus, we are now the elect. You have been elected and chosen because of the foreknowledge God has of you giving you're life to Jesus Christ. Romans 8:29 says, *"For those God foreknew he also predestined to be conformed to the likeness of his Son, that he might be the firstborn among many brothers"*. The Lord foreknew, or knew beforehand, who would choose life and who would choose death. In this way, the saved are elect and chosen. Revelation 17:14 (NKJV) reads, *"These will make war with the Lamb, and the Lamb will overcome them, for He is Lord of lords and King of kings; and those who are with Him are called, chosen, and faithful."* Those who are with the King are the called and chosen ones because they chose to be with Him. They responded to the call.

Acts 13:44-46 clarifies this.

> *On the next Sabbath almost the whole city gathered to hear the word of the Lord. When the Jews saw the crowds, they were filled with jealousy and talked abusively against what Paul was saying. Then Paul and Barnabas answered them boldly: "We had to speak the word of God to you first. Since you reject it and do not consider yourselves worthy of eternal life, we now turn to the Gentiles."*

There is much to be said in this passage. First of all, the Jews Paul and Barnabas are speaking to, thought they were the "elect", that they were the "chosen" ones of God. But Paul tells them that they did not consider themselves worthy of eternal life and that they rejected God. It doesn't say God rejected them and so they are condemned. Paul and Barnabas were sent to them first to proclaim the good news, but they rejected it and so chose for themselves their eternal destination. It confirms the scripture that says, *"Therefore let him who thinks he stands take **heed** lest he fall"* (1 Corinthians 10:12). John also writes of this phenomenon when he says,

> *He was in the world, and though the world was made through him, the world did not recognize him. He came to that which was his own, but his own did not receive him. Yet to all who received him, to those who believed in his name, he gave the right to become children of God – children born not of natural descent, nor of*

human decision or a husband's will, but born of God. (John
1:10-13)

Even angels were not spared when they rejected Christ, as Peter writes,
*"For if God did not spare angels when they sinned, but sent them to hell,
putting them into gloomy dungeons to be held for judgment. . . "* (2 Peter
2:4). If election as taught in some circles were true, then God in His
sovereignty would have made the angels sin, then punished them. That
would mean He made Lucifer and the angels (1/3 of them) so He could
lose them to evil. Not only does that sound strange, but totally unlike the
way God describes Himself in the Bible.

A real-life illustration of the deceitfulness of this teaching is what started
the writing of the book. Recently I (Tiffany) was interviewing a pastor
and was shocked by his response to a question I asked him about
salvation. He said that he believed Jesus didn't actually die for the world,
but only for a select few people. I questioned why then would he bother
evangelizing? If people were predestined in the way that he described,
what would be the point of trying to spread the gospel? Either people
were created to be saved or be damned, so why bother with the great
commission? He replied that it was out of obedience to the command to
go out into all the world, that we were supposed to be evangelizing. We're
just supposed to be obedient. The whole idea struck me as absolutely
ludicrous. My God is not a time-waster. Neither, did He make me to be
one. If everyone didn't have an equal chance to be saved, there was no
point in trying to save them.

However, I didn't want to assume anything. So, I went before the LORD
in listening prayer, and the verses against the theologies described above
just kept coming to me. It was amazing. Almost every time I opened my
Bible, God showed me more scriptures that show how much He loves the
world, and what exactly Jesus accomplished on the cross. Additionally,
I spoke with Kirk about this. He too listened and the LORD revealed
Truth to him as well through the Word. So consequently, we have listened

to the Lord on these issues and been in deep study of the Word. A person cannot go wrong by reading the Bible with a mind bound to Jesus Christ. However, there are people who refuse to believe the Bible, though they say they believe it. In reality, they believe a theology. Their view of the Word is distorted as they look through the lens of their theology and try fit the Word into it. The Holy Spirit is the author and must be consulted to be led into all truth, not a theory or a study by man.

Sometimes we believe our experiences more than the Word. This requires much less faith and wrestling with God. For example, in discussing healing and God's will to heal, one of the many reasons we believe it really is God's will to heal people is this: we look at the ministry of Jesus Christ. He healed everyone who came to Him, never turned anyone away, never said, "Well you are in a trial so come back next week then I can heal you." None of those things... and Christ is the perfect representation of God. (Heb. 1:3)

So, we need to look at where Jesus ministered. He spent His time almost exclusively with the sinners - the people one would expect <u>not</u> to be the elect. We would expect the religious people to be the elect because of their actions and outward appearance. The Pharisees thought any other theology beside theirs was wrong. They thought they were the elect. We all tend to think this way to one degree or another. But, Jesus has one body, not several. Even though Jesus railed on the Pharisees relentlessly, He still took the time to explain how to be born again to Nicodemus. He explains how to be saved using the words of John 3:16. *"For God so loved the world, that He gave His one and only Son that whoever believes in Him should not perish but have eternal life."* That is what this book is about. It's about the love of God and what Jesus, the King, has done.

God makes His truth very clear in 1 Peter 1:2. It reads,

> *. . . elect according to the foreknowledge of God the Father, in sanctification of the Spirit, for obedience and sprinkling of the blood of Jesus Christ: Grace to you and peace be multiplied.* (NKJV)

Obviously the elect are the chosen because of foreknowledge. God knew beforehand who would choose life and who would choose death. Joshua, way back in the Old Testament tells us to make a choice. He says to choose life or death and then goes on to let us know what his choice is – life!

We are also exhorted to make our calling and election sure (see 2 Peter 1:5-11). If we were not to have any say in our acceptance of the gospel, this would be totally unnecessary.

The Pharisees certainly thought they knew where they stood, yet they were the ones who were in the most danger. Luke tells us that

> *All the people, even the tax collectors, when they heard Jesus' words, acknowledged that God's way was right, because they had been baptized by John. But the Pharisees and experts in the law rejected God's purpose for themselves, because they had not been baptized by John.* (Luke 7:29-30)

Because the Pharisees thought they knew better, they would not repent and be baptized by John. And they would not believe Jesus. In fact, they rejected Him, the One who came to save them. Luke says they rejected God's purpose for them, their salvation, and the "good plans" we read about in the book of Jeremiah. *"Knowledge puffs up, but love builds up"* (1 Corinthians 8:1). They had a lot of knowledge, but did not have love.

Jesus later rebukes the teachers of the law for not only rejecting Him, but causing others to reject Him as well. He says, *"Woe to you experts in the law, because you have taken away the key to knowledge. You yourselves have not entered, and you have hindered those who were entering"* (Luke 11:52). It is obvious that the LORD wanted these people being hindered to enter the kingdom of God. That is why he says "woe" to the teachers of the law. They were hindering others from entering the Kingdom of Heaven. This is what is meant in Matthew when Jesus says, *"Not everyone who says to me, 'Lord, Lord,' will enter the kingdom of heaven, but only he who does the will of my Father who is in heaven"* (Matthew 7:21-23). And what is God's will? It is to *"believe in the one he has sent"* (John 6:20).

There is a choice here. We either do the will of the Father, or we don't. Jesus says that calling him "Lord" isn't enough. We actually have to do the Father's will to be saved. This means we have to do something in order to receive the gift of salvation. Because someone doesn't believe, that person is condemned "already". (*"Whoever believes in him is not condemned, but whoever does not believe stands condemned already because he has not believed in the name of God's one and only Son"* John 3:18.) This shows God's foreknowledge, but has no indication that God created that person just so he or she would go to hell. The Word tells us clearly that Jesus died for us all and we need to choose life, not death.

First Peter 3:18 (TNIV) reads, *"For Christ also suffered once for sins, the righteous for the unrighteous, to bring you to God. He was put to death in the body but made alive in the Spirit."* This passage says, "the righteous for the unrighteous, to bring YOU to God". Who is "you"? It is everyone who believes. If the choice of salvation was made for you, there would be no need to be "brought" to God. It simply wouldn't be necessary.

Another passage that speaks of Jesus' intercession is 1 Peter 2:24: *"He himself bore our sins in his body on the tree, so that we might die to sins and live for righteousness; by his wounds you have been healed."* He bore "our" sins and by His stripes you (meaning everyone who believes) have been healed. He interceded for us, something that wouldn't be needed if we were simply chosen/elected before time to go to glory.

In John 17:20-23 Jesus prays,

> *I pray also for those who will believe in me through their message, that all of them may be one, Father, just as you are in me and I am in you. May they also be in us so that the world may believe that you have sent me. I have given them the glory that you gave me,*

that they may be one as we are one: I in them and you in me. May
they be brought to complete unity to let the world know that you
sent me and have loved them even as you have loved me.

This prayer from the LORD is specific in saying that it is those who will believe in Him that will be saved and it is those people that He is praying for. He knows who will believe in Him, but there is no indication whatsoever that those who believe have no say in the matter. However, there is every indication that those who believe, have to do just that to be saved – they have to believe.

To have a real argument for election (meaning God chose some people for hell and some for heaven, and people have no say in the matter), one would need to believe that God even caused the fall of man because He knew when He created earth that man would sin. However, we know that God cannot do evil. Rick Joyner writes in *Overcoming Confusion,* "God did not cause man to Fall – that was man's choice, but it will serve to allow him to be exalted to the high place of being the abode of God, because we will forever have reason to fully understand our need and dependence on His grace and redemption" (p. 53). Indeed, God didn't cause the fall of mankind, nor does He cause people to choose hell. Instead, He implores them to choose life, and like Joshua, we must decide this day whom we will serve.

In 1 Corinthians 10, Paul speaks to the church at Corinth and tells them that even though they have freedom to do certain things, they need to abstain from that freedom for the sake of others. He says, *"Give no offense, either to the Jews or to the Greeks or to the church of God, just as I also please all men in all things, not seeking my own profit, but the profit of many, that they may be saved"* (1 Corinthians 10:32-33, NKJV). If everyone was already predestined to go to heaven or hell, there would be no need to act the way Paul tells us to act, because either people would believe or they wouldn't. They would have no say in the matter at all.

Many examples are given of people responding to the gospel, believing in Christ, and being saved. The household of Cornelius is a good example of this.

> *"He [Peter] will bring you a message through which you and all your household will be saved." As I began to speak, the Holy Spirit came on them as he had come on us at the beginning. Then I remembered what the Lord had said: "John baptized with water, but you will be baptized with the Holy Spirit." So if God gave the same gift as he gave us, who believed in the Lord Jesus Christ, who was I to think that I could oppose God?* (Acts 11:14-17)

These people at Cornelius' house were saved through the message spoken to them. The Word is Jesus Christ. Cornelius' household was saved because they believed and they were baptized in the Holy Spirit, and then were baptized in water.

The jailer is another example of this "believing and being saved" phenomenon. *"He then brought them out an asked, 'Sirs, what must I do to be saved?' They replied, 'Believe in the Lord Jesus, and you will be saved – you and your household.'"* (Acts 16:30-31)

This is very straightforward. The jailer asks how he can be saved, and he is told that he and his household must believe and they will be saved. It's simple. We tend to make things more complicated than they are as we attempt to put God into our theological boxes.

> *For God did not send his Son into the world to condemn the world, but to save the world through him. Whoever believes in him is not condemned, but whoever does not believe stands condemned already because he has not believed in the name of God's one and only Son.* (John 3:17-18 NIV)

Those who do not believe are "already" condemned because they did not believe in Jesus. This is Jesus speaking in these verses. He is telling the people that if they do not believe, then they stand condemned.

When Jesus speaks or acts, He is showing the way to eternal life (John 12:50). There is always a choice set before us. We were created with free will to choose life or death.

> *As for the person who hears my words but does not keep them, I do not judge him. For I did not come to judge the world, but to save it. There is a judge for the one who rejects me and does not accept my words; that very word which I spoke will condemn him at the last day.* (John 12:47-48 NIV).

Let's not be one of those who will be condemned because they rejected Jesus. Let us instead be of those who seek Jesus and find Him.

"*I love them that love me; and those that seek me early shall find me*" (Proverbs 8:17, KJV). It's too late after Christ comes again or when we're standing before the Judgment Seat to choose Christ. We need to seek Him now, while it is still "today" and the promise is that we will find Him. This is a good promise, for we know that all the promises of God are yes in Christ and in Him Amen to the glory of God through us (2 Corinthians 1:20). Praise be to God!

CHAPTER 6

Faith Like a Child

If you have children, you may remember when they were the age in which they believed everything you said. They believed you because you loved them, and they trusted you because they looked up to you. You were the person with whom they wanted to spend their time. You were who they wanted to impress. You were who they looked to for wisdom and answers. Your children had faith in you. Hopefully, you've been able to keep that faith with your children if they are older now by being honest and trustworthy, reliable, and wise. We are to be like children and believe our Father God in everything He says, including the way to salvation, just like children believe their parents in everything when they are young.

The Bible says we are supposed to have faith like a child to be saved. If the Gospel is easy enough for a child to understand it, we can be sure complicated messages are erroneous. We believe and we are saved, any additions or subtractions are error. God says in 2 Corinthians 11:3, *"But I fear, lest somehow, as the serpent deceived Eve by his craftiness, so your minds may be corrupted from the simplicity that is in Christ" (NKJV)*. There is a child-like simplicity to the message of salvation. That doesn't mean God is simple, but the message of salvation surely is. We need to be like children and just believe it.

FOR GOD SO LOVED THE WORLD

Matthew 18:3 says, *"I tell you the truth, unless you change and become like little children, you will never enter the kingdom of heaven."* God's calling people to change. He tells us we have to be like children in order to enter the kingdom of heaven. If we didn't need to do this - if our salvation were determined without us having a choice, this would not be necessary. God would say, "Hey, stay the same way you are because I either created you for heaven or for hell and it really doesn't matter what you do." But, God doesn't say that. He tells us to be like children. Children believe whatever you tell them. They don't understand that we adults say things we don't really mean sometimes. Once they start to grasp that we don't always tell the complete truth, that's when their faith starts to diminish. It's a sad reality. We're not keepers of our word like God is. His word never fails. Ours does. When we fail to follow through with what we say to our children, they start to doubt that God will follow through as well. That's why Jesus said, *"Let the little children come to me, and do not hinder them, for the kingdom of heaven belongs to such as these"* (Matthew 19:14).

The faith of a child is amazing. We'll give you an example. I (Tiffany) had learned that God gave His believers authority over the enemy and that sickness was paid for at the cross (Isa 53:4-5, 1 Peter 2:4, etc.). So, I had been trying to teach my little children how to pray with authority. One day, I had the hiccups off and on all day. It was starting to be a nuisance. So, I complained to my four-year-old son, William. I said, "I've had these hiccups all day, ugh!" To which he yelled, "Tell them to go away!" I was surprised, but took the correction from my boy, and yelled, "Hiccups go away in Jesus name!" They stopped immediately. This is the faith of a child. My son believed they would go away because he believed our authority in Christ more than I did. The Truth had gotten past his head, and into his heart. It's the same with salvation.

When we don't follow through on what we say, and when we teach our children man-made doctrines, we pick away at their faith until they're just as unbelieving and doubtful as we are. Mark 10:14b-15 says,

Let the little children come to me, and do not hinder them, for the kingdom of God belongs to such as these. I tell you the truth, anyone who will not receive the kingdom of God like a child will never enter it. (See Luke 18:16-17 for the same scenario.)

We're commanded not to hinder our children, but to be like them. We're told to believe like they believe and we too will enter the kingdom of the One we love. It is humbling to become like children. It seems like foolishness to the world to believe in a God we can't even see. But, that's exactly what we are to do. We are to believe EVERYTHING He says, even if what we see with our physical eyes does not line up with what His Word says is Truth.

Matthew chapter 18 goes into detail about the faith of children. Jesus had a little child stand among him and his disciples and he said:

I tell you the truth, unless you change and become like little children, you will never enter the kingdom of heaven. Therefore, whoever humbles himself like this child is the greatest in the kingdom of heaven.

And whoever welcomes a little child like this in my name welcomes me. But if anyone causes one of these little ones who believe in me to sin, it would be better for him to have a large millstone hung around his neck and to be drowned in the depths of the sea.

***

See that you do not look down on one of these little ones. For I tell you that their angels in heaven always see the face of my Father in heaven.

What do you think? If a man owns a hundred sheep, and one of them wanders away, will he not leave the ninety-nine on the hills and go to look for the one that wandered off? And if he finds it, I

47

tell you the truth, he is happier about that one sheep than about the ninety-nine that did not wander off. In the same way your Father in heaven is not willing that any of these little ones should be lost. (Matthew 18:3-6, 10-14)

First Jesus tells his disciples and the others listening that if we don't become like children, we will not enter the Kingdom of Heaven. That takes humility. Children ask questions. They don't act like they have all the answers. They are very teachable and desire to learn. Children look up to people more mature than themselves, and they're not afraid to make mistakes. They also are not afraid to serve. They don't believe a job is beneath them.

Secondly, Jesus puts a lot of weight on our treatment of children. He says that if we cause them to sin, it'd be better to die. And He warns us that children's angels always see the face of the Father. God knows how we treat the most vulnerable in society, and we are held accountable for it. We're told to not only treat them well, but to be like them. It is humbling.

Lastly, God makes it very clear in this passage that He does not desire any of His sheep to be lost. He wants all to be saved, and we need to make that a priority too.

The writer of Hebrews tells us the reason some are not saved: *"the word which they heard did not profit them, not being mixed with faith in those who heard it"* (Hebrews 4:2 NKJV). It is God's desire to save everyone, but not everyone will believe. They hear the Word, but it doesn't profit them by saving them because they don't have faith like a child to believe it.

It is the power of God in Christ that saves us, but that saving is through faith as we read in Ephesians. *"For it is by grace you have been saved, through faith – and this not from yourselves, it is the gift of God – not by works, so that no one can boast"* (Ephesians 2:8-9). This grace comes through faith. We need to believe deep within ourselves. It's more than head acknowledgement, but a persuasion of the heart.

We need faith for salvation. Romans 5:1-2 says, *"Therefore, since we have been justified through faith, we have peace with God through our Lord Jesus Christ, through whom we have gained access by faith into this grace in which we now stand."* We gain access to grace by faith. We have to believe God.

There's a wonderful story about a woman who came to a Pharisee's house where Jesus was dining. She was so moved in her spirit that she cried hard enough to be able to wash Jesus' feet with her tears and then dry them with her hair. (You can read the whole story in Luke 7:36-50.) Jesus explained to the judgmental Pharisees that it was because this woman was forgiven so much that she was willing to show so much love. She really humiliated herself in front of these dinner guests and because she humbled herself in repentance and gratitude, she was able to hear, *"Your sins are forgiven"* (v. 48). Not only that, but Jesus said to her, *"Your faith has saved you. Go in peace"* (v. 50 NKJV). It wasn't this woman's good works, but it was her faith in Jesus Christ that saved her. She showed her faith by what she did, but Jesus is the only one recorded in Scripture that understood what she was doing and why. Jesus commends her faith, just as He does the little children that come to Him.

As Jesus commends the faith of children to his disciples after He rebuked the disciples for not allowing the children to come to Him, He says, *"I tell you the truth, anyone who will not receive the kingdom of God like a little child will never enter it"* (Mark 10:15). The choice word here is "receive." The gift of God found in Jesus Christ has to be received through faith.

John Bevere puts it well in his book *Drawing Near*: He writes, "Everything we receive from the Lord is through faith. There is a truth I've discovered that many in the body of Christ are ignorant of, and that is, God does not respond to our need, He responds to our faith!" (p. 210) How true this is. It's foolish and lazy to assume that since God knows your needs, He will automatically respond by giving you what you need. He desires to communicate with us and desires us to ask Him for what we need. However, even asking for what we need takes faith because we need to believe that He will respond when we ask. We are His children and He tells us that He's a better parent than we are, and even we give good things to our children when they ask for it.

Bevere goes on to say, "God expects us to know His will, for we are told, 'Therefore do not be unwise, but understand what the will of the Lord is' (Eph. 5:17); then once we know it, ask with faith and confidence." (p. 213) Faith is necessary because *everything that does not come from faith is sin*" (Romans 14:23).

When you come to God in faith and hope, it is more than an "I hope He hears me and answers me" attitude you must have. Hope is a "confident expectation"; whereas, our word for hope is a "maybe so" hope (p. 213).

> People are easily distracted because they hope they will connect with God when drawing near. No, you must believe *He is*, you must believe *He is* there; you must believe that *He is* listening and will respond; and He deserves your undivided attention. Faith gives the assurance that *He is* giving you His full attention, because you know He has promised, and He cannot lie; if you draw near, He in turn will come close. (Bevere p. 214)

John Bevere is talking about drawing near to God in the above statement, but it holds true to every time we come before the Lord. We must come in faith. We must believe He hears us and desires to answer us. We must believe He wants us to be saved in every way. We must believe He is love. We must believe it with more than our heads, but our hearts as well. If you are a loving parent, your child believes you love them and will watch out for them in every situation. They believe this truth with more than mere mental assent, but with their whole beings. This is how we need to approach our Father. We need to come to Him, climb in His lap, and humbly ask for what we need. He is great. He is good. He is just. He is holy. He desires to hold you and listen and He desires you to be saved, for He wants you to be with Him in eternity. He desires closeness with you, and that closeness takes faith.

Bevere gives an example from King Saul's life about the need for faith. He writes, "If you . . . follow Saul's life you will notice a steady deterioration of his faith. You will also notice he progressively becomes more distant from the Lord. His intimacy level wanes because of the fact that our ability to have intimacy with God is directly proportional to our faith. In regard to this the apostle John says,

> *This is how we will be confident in God's presence. If our conscience condemns us, we know that God is greater than our conscience and that he knows everything. And so, my dear friends, if our conscience does not condemn us, we have courage in God's presence.* (John 3:19-22 TEV)" (p. 220)

We have courage to go to God for what we need and what we want in faith.

As a side note, we do not believe that children unable to choose Christ for themselves are sent to hell. That theory goes against the very nature of God for God is love and also just. Neither attribute of God would allow a precious child unable to choose life or death to spend eternity in hell. But, when each child reaches an age of understanding and is able to choose, they need to choose Christ. Each child's age of understanding is different, and we do not need to be legalistic on this point.

CHAPTER 7

Power of Prayer

Prayer matters. James says that the prayers of a person right with God are powerful and effective (see James Chapter Five). There are many passages of scripture that testify to the power of prayer. Dutch Sheets has written several excellent books on this topic. We would recommend that you read those if you need some convincing in this area. Specifically, the book *How to Pray for Lost Loved Ones* would be a good choice as the topic relates to salvation.

We are lulled into a spiritual stupor when we believe that "whatever will be, will be;" or "what's going to happen will happen." That is foolishness, and an effective tactic the enemy uses to get you to be ineffective in the Kingdom of Heaven. If the devil can get you to believe that your prayers don't really make a difference, then you will not be praying in faith, which is what moves mountains, and you may even give up praying entirely. Or if you do pray, you will do it out of some sort of religious duty.

Mark 6:1-12 reads,

> *Jesus left there and went to his hometown, accompanied by his disciples. When the Sabbath came, he began to teach in the synagogue, and many who heard him were amazed.*

"Where did this man get these things?" they asked. "What's this wisdom that has been given him, that he even does miracles! Isn't this the carpenter? Isn't this Mary's son and the brother of James, Joseph, Judas and Simon? Aren't his sisters here with us?" And they took offense at him.

Jesus said to them, "Only in his hometown, among his relatives and in his own house is a prophet without honor." He could not do any miracles there, except lay his hands on a few sick people and heal them. And he was amazed at their lack of faith.

Then Jesus went around teaching from village to village. Calling the Twelve to him, he sent them out two by two and gave them authority over evil spirits. These were his instructions: "Take nothing for the journey except a staff—no bread, no bag, no money in your belts. Wear sandals but not an extra tunic. Whenever you enter a house, stay there until you leave that town. And if any place will not welcome you or listen to you, shake the dust off your feet when you leave, as a testimony against them."

They went out and preached that people should repent.

Here we see a number of things. The first thing we should notice is that Jesus Himself "could not do any miracles there". Wow! So what can we anticipate in a place where we don't expect much from prayer? Not much.

Another thing to notice is that they were offended at Jesus because they knew Him growing up. He wasn't a scribe or a Pharisee. In today's terms, we might say, "Where did he get this knowledge? He didn't go to seminary. Isn't he just a mechanic or she just a home maker? We know their parents! They shouldn't be believed because they don't have a degree and are not pastors or even elders or deacons." Yet we see that Jesus taught His disciples for a very short time before He gave them authority to cast out demons and preach and teach. God even tells us that if we are filled with the Holy Spirit we do not need anyone to teach us because the Holy Spirit will lead us into all Truth. He says,

> *As for you, the anointing you received from him remains on you, and you do not need anyone to teach you. But as his anointing teaches you about all things and as that anointing is real, not counterfeit – just as it has taught you, remain in him.* (1 John 2:27)

The catch here of course is to remain in the vine, Jesus Christ. When we try to do things through our own strength and knowledge, we will stray and ultimately fail. We should not be offended by the occupation of the person God has chosen to bring the truth, even if he or she does not have a degree, the title of Pastor, or any other criteria for a "teacher" we believe he or she should have. Our unbelief will stop what God wants to do through that particular servant of God.

Right after Jesus goes to His hometown and is rejected, He sends out His disciples and tells them that if they are rejected, they are to leave where they were sent to minister and go elsewhere. If there was unbelief at a place where they stopped, they were to shake the dust off their feet and split town. They were to stay for a time, and if they and their message were rejected, they were to leave and feel no remorse. This is called justice. Our God is just. When we reject Him in unbelief, believing that our prayers are ineffective, He will shake the dust off His feet as He leaves. Jesus only did what He saw His Father doing, so obviously this is how God feels when He's rejected. It's another reason we really do need to choose who we will serve.

Why is it that when there is a special performance such as a musical or drama at church, people flock to the event? However, if there's a prayer meeting, there's generally only a handful of people there? It is because people really do not expect much from their prayers. They are not praying in faith because if we pray in faith, we wait expectantly for what we prayed for to happen. *"Faith is the substance of things hoped for, the evidence of things not seen" (Hebrews 11:1, NKJV).* God is looking for people to pray. He's looking for intercessors! He says, *"I looked for someone among them who would build up the wall and stand before me in the gap on behalf of the land so I would not have to destroy it, but I found no one." (Ezekiel 22:30)* Your prayers make a difference. God wants people to intercede. This is how He wants to work. We intercede and He moves. He can move without us, but He desires to work with us.

We need to care and stop being apathetic. Judgment begins with the house of God, and even the pagans/unbelievers know when something is wrong, and they implore us to call on our God for help (1Peter 4:17). Rick Joyner writes,

> Just as the heathen had to wake up Jonah and convince him to call on his God, in many ways even the heathen are doing this today. On every front, problems are beyond human remedy, and they are starting to understand this.

> Many kinds of judgment are in Scripture—one is condemnation and one is destruction, but the rest are discipline from the Lord. As we are told in Hebrews 12, the Lord disciplines those whom He loves. Therefore, the judgments we are suffering [in the United States] are because He loves us, and He is seeking to turn us back from the path of destruction we are on. This judgment has to start with His own people because how can He judge the nations for the things that even His own people are doing?

> We must remember that the path to having our land healed begins with God's people humbling themselves. Our declarations against the evil deeds of our leaders, or the people, will not come with outrage and anger as much as an appeal seasoned with humility. We must always keep in mind that "God resists the proud, but gives grace to the humble" (James 4:6 NKJV).

(Rick Joyner's Word for the Week / Prepared for the Times, part 22)

Prayer is essential. The devil has veiled the eyes of people's hearts, and only the Holy Spirit can open them. And we know that the Holy Spirit moves when we pray. *"But even if our gospel is veiled, it is veiled to those who are perishing, whose minds the god of this age has blinded, who do not believe, lest the light of the gospel of the glory of Christ, who is the image of God, should shine on them"* (2 Corinithians 4:3-4 NKJV). The LORD is not blinding people, but the devil is (the god of this age).

Do we really believe our prayers are powerful and effective like God says in the book of James? If God is Truth, He cannot lie, which means that what He says is always true. We have to pray against the veil over unbelievers' eyes. The devil wouldn't have any need of blinding people's eyes if their salvation wasn't a battle. If God created people strictly to send them to hell, why would there be any need to fight for souls? Why would the devil fight so hard to gain souls for hell? There wouldn't be a need.

Second Timothy 2:26 (NKJV) tells us that one of the reasons we pray is so that people will *"come to their senses and escape the snare of the devil, having been taken captive by him to do his will."* Our God is not a time-waster. He's not out to make us evangelize and spend time praying for souls if it's not going to matter. There's a battle raging and we're supposed to be fighting it. Jesus took the fall for the world, so there is power behind our prayers because the Holy Spirit lives in us. Our prayers offered in faith are effective.

Second Corinthians 4:13 (NKJV) says, *"And since we have the same spirit of faith, according to what is written, 'I believed and therefore I spoke,' we also believe and therefore speak."* Speak. Use your voice that was created in the image of God. Take the authority Christ gave you, and watch His Kingdom come.

Jesus says in John 6, *"No one can come to me unless the Father who sent me draws him, and I will raise him up at the last day"* (v. 44). It is true that the Father draws us to Him through the Holy Spirit. This is why we pray. God can draw someone to Himself by Himself, but He will also do it through intercession. We need to be praying for the lost. Many people are invited, but few are chosen (Matthew 22:14). It is those who believe who are chosen. John 1:12-13 reads, *"But as many as received Him, to them He gave the right to become children of God, to those who believe in His name: who were born, not of blood, nor of the will of the flesh, nor of the will of man, but of God."* We are chosen when we clothe ourselves with the righteousness of Christ, when we trust in Jesus. Even people that do not make a choice, end up choosing. No choice equals choosing death, not life.

Additionally, Jesus says that when He is "lifted up from the earth, [He] will draw all people" to himself (John 12:32). He draws everyone to Himself; "all people" means everyone. Some will still resist, which is why we need to be in battle through prayer for the lost.

John Bevere in his book *Drawing Near (pgs. 24-25)* explains the necessity of prayer for salvation in a very clear way. He writes,

> Jesus Himself tells us, "No one can come to Me unless the Father who sent Me draws him" (John 6:44). This is why intercession for others who don't have a relationship with God through Jesus is so critical. Even though God "desires all men to be saved and to come to the knowledge of the truth" (1 Tim. 2:4), and has pursued this end consistently throughout history, He still wants His children to catch His passion for the lost and cry out to Him on their behalf. For this reason Jesus said, "The harvest is plentiful, but the laborers are few. Therefore, pray the Lord of the harvest to send out laborers into His harvest" (Matt. 9:37-38).

This is why we pray. We need the heart of God for the lost. Send the laborers into the harvest field, Oh Lord, send them. Send me!

CHAPTER 8

Faith Alone?

You believe that there is one God. Good! Even the
demons believe that—and shudder. (James 2:19)

Did you know that belief in the existence of God is not going to get you into heaven? A mental assent that God is real is not enough. The Lord says that even the demons believe there is one God, yet they are going to spend eternity in hell. Romans 1:16-17 says,

> *For I am not ashamed of the gospel of Christ, for it is the power of*
> *God to salvation for everyone who believes, for the Jew first and*
> *also for the Greek. For in it the righteousness of God is revealed*
> *from faith to faith; as it is written, "The just shall live by faith."*
> (NKJV)

So, what does it mean to "live by faith." Hebrews 11:1 (NKJV) says, *"Now faith is the substance of things hoped for, the evidence of things not seen."* That means our faith has substance. It has to be more than a mental agreement to something.

There is an aspect of salvation called "obedience." Jesus says that those who obey him are the ones who love him. The writer of Hebrews tells us Jesus "became the author of eternal salvation to all who obey Him" (Hebrews 5:9 NKJV).

There's an interesting parable Jesus tells in Luke. It is about the faith of a mustard seed and then Jesus goes right into the story of a servant and his master. The two do not initially seem to fit, until the Spirit brings understanding to the passage.

> *He replied, "If you have faith as small as a mustard seed, you can say to this mulberry tree, 'Be uprooted and planted in the sea,' and it will obey you.*
>
> *Suppose one of you had a servant plowing or looking after sheep. Would he say to the servant when he comes in from the field, 'Come along now and sit down to eat'? Would he not rather say, 'Prepare my supper, get yourself ready and wait on me while I eat and drink; after that you may eat and drink'? Would he thank the servant because he did what he was told to do? So you also, when you have done everything you were told to do, should say, 'We are unworthy servants; we have only done our duty.'"* (Luke 17:6-10)

Referring to this passage, John Bevere writes,

> Why does a servant farm or tend flocks for his master? The ultimate goal is to get food on his table. What Jesus is asking is: Why would a servant tend crops or flocks, then come in and not finish the job by putting the food on his master's table? To be successful he needs to complete *all* of what he has been asked to do. Not finishing could be compared to having a seed that you plant, water, and fertilize; but just before it comes to the time of harvest, you destroy it or out of neglect allow the fruit to rot.

> Jesus is speaking of our obedience to Him . . . [W]e must be
> obedient servants in all we are asked to do . . . and that is the key
> to seeing our faith increase. (*Drawing Near*, p. 218)

So obedience leads to greater faith. We listen and obey, and the next
time we listen and obey again. As time goes on, we get better at listening
and obeying, and our faith increases as we are better able to discern the
LORD's voice.

Isaiah 29:13 reads, *"The Lord says: 'These people come near to me with
their mouth and honor me with their lips, but their hearts are far from me.
Their worship is made up only of rules taught by men.'"* God obviously
wants more than an acknowledgement of Him. He wants a heart motive
that manifests itself in obedience. Bevere states it well in *Drawing Near*.
He says that "the fear of the Lord begins in the heart and manifests itself
in our outward actions" (p. 70). There's more to it than just believing or
saying we have faith or have the fear of the Lord. What we believe in our
hearts will show itself, and by our fruits we shall be known. The apostle
John writes, *"Dear children, let us not love with words or tongue but with
actions and in truth"* (1 John 3:18).

This is something David and Solomon were commended and blessed for
doing (showing by their actions that they loved the Lord). First Kings
3:3 says, *"Solomon showed his love for the LORD by walking according
to the statutes of his father David . . ."*. Solomon's actions proved his love
for the Lord. His faith and actions were working together.

A few verses later we're told, *"Solomon answered [God], 'You have shown
great kindness to your servant, my father David, because he was faithful to
you and righteous and upright in heart'"* (1 Kings 3:6). Why was David
shown such great "kindness"? It was because he was faithful to God,
righteous, and upright in heart. He was known as a man after God's own
heart. His faith and actions worked together.

In John 5:24-29 Jesus says,

> *I tell you the truth, whoever hears my word and believes him who sent me has eternal life and will not be condemned; he has crossed over from death to life. I tell you the truth, a time is coming and has now come when the dead will hear the voice of the Son of God and those who hear will live. For as the Father has life in himself, so he has granted the Son to have life in himself. And he has given him authority to judge because he is the Son of Man.*
>
> *Do not be amazed at this, for a time is coming when all who are in their graves will hear his voice and come out – those who have done good will rise to live, and those who have done evil will rise to be condemned.*

The Lord says we must believe and do good. In other words, if we believe, our actions will follow our beliefs. We will do the good God prepared in advance for us to do.

Later on the people ask Jesus, *"What must we do to do the works God requires?"* Jesus answered, *"The work of God is this: to believe in the one he has sent"* (John 6:28-29). This belief requires action. Faith without works is dead, as James tells us. However, this also means to rest in Jesus' finished work. He accomplished it, now we go out with authority and take back the ground the devil stole.

Faith in Jesus Christ is certainly what we need to enter heaven. So then what kind of faith is this that we need? It is certainly not a simple historical faith that Jesus once existed. It is faith that will produce works. After all how can real faith <u>not</u> produce works? If Jesus is the true shepherd and we, as His sheep, hear His voice, simple obedience will produce works. Following Him as a sheep follows a shepherd is actively doing something.

John 10:27 says, *"My sheep listen to my voice; I know them, and they follow me."* If we are followers of Jesus, we need to be hearing His voice. We need to recognize it and be obedient to it. Jesus says that we listen to Him and then follow Him. That means we do more than just hear what He says. We actually have to obey what He says to do. Jesus tells us a few chapters later in John 14:23 that *"Anyone who loves me will obey my teaching. My Father will love them, and we will come to them and make our home with them."* That's an awesome promise. God Himself makes His home with those who obey Him. Only those who obey Him actually love Him. Obedience is the litmus test for loving God. Do we obey Him?

It is very dangerous to believe that we have no responsibility to believe. There's a belief out there that says that God gives us faith, so we can do nothing – we can only believe if God gives us faith to believe. While it is true that there is a gift of the Holy Spirit called the Gift of Faith, that is all together different from believing God and having saving faith. God does gift us all with faith, but it's up to us to act upon that faith. True belief requires action. Lack of action shows doubt. That is why we cannot separate faith from obedience. If we believe God, we will obey Him.

A. W. Tozer says the following in *Paths to Power*

> In the New Testament there is no contradiction between faith and obedience. Between faith and law-works, yes; between law and grace, yes; but between faith and obedience, not at all. The Bible recognizes no faith that does not lead to obedience, nor does it recognize any obedience that does not spring from faith. . . The trouble with many of us today is that we are trying to believe without intending to obey. [B]elief has been robbed of its moral content and made to be little more than an assent to gospel truth. (pp. 24-26)

Let us believe with more than mental assent, but with our actions as well.

It was asked of Jesus, *"What shall we do, that we may work the works of God?"* Jesus answered and said to them, *"This is the work of God, that you believe in Him whom He sent."* (John 6:28-29 NKJV) This is the work we are to do. We are to believe God. Believing Him is more than a mental assent, but requires action. If we really believe what He says is Truth, we will follow through on what He says. For example, Noah really believed God would flood the earth. So, he did what God said to do. Likewise, if we really believe God only speaks the truth, we will do as he says and lay our hands on the sick and they will recover, we will cast out demons, etc.

What kinds of things could we expect to see in disciples who are obedient? What would our job description look like? Jesus tells us in Matthew 10:8, "Heal the sick, raise the dead, cleanse those who have leprosy, drive out demons. Freely you have received, freely give." These are the things we ought to be doing.

Compassion and love were demonstrated by Christ as He healed, performed miracles, and cast out demons. These parts of the ministry of Christ (healing, deliverance, miracles) consumed more of His ministry time here on earth than anything else He did. The fruit and gifts of the Spirit are graphically depicted in the life of Christ. We would do well to follow His lead.

How can anyone say that they are a "Christ follower" and not spend a similar amount of time doing the things He actually did? Why has our theology and doctrine taken precedence over the things that Christ actually did?

We know that we have come to know him if we keep his commands. Those who say, "I know him," but do not do what he commands are liars, and the truth is not in them. But if anyone obeys his word, love for God is truly made complete in them. This is how we know we are in him: <u>Whoever claims to live in him must live as Jesus did</u>.

Dear friends, I am not writing you a new command but an old one, which you have had since the beginning. This old command is the message you have heard. Yet I am writing you a new command; its truth is seen in him and in you, because the darkness is passing and the true light is already shining.

Those who claim to be in the light but hate a fellow believer are still in the darkness. Those who love their fellow believers live in the light, and there is nothing in them to make them stumble. But those who hate a fellow believer are in the darkness and walk around in the darkness; they do not know where they are going, because the darkness has blinded them. (1 John 2:3-11 TNIV)

We do not want to follow man's wisdom in this book. However, the Lord has given us many quotes to use, and this quote is rather pointed regarding this topic.

The matter is quite simple. The bible is very easy to understand. But we Christians are a bunch of scheming swindlers. We pretend to be unable to understand it because we know very well that the minute we understand, we are obliged to act accordingly. Take any words in the New Testament and forget everything except pledging yourself to act accordingly. My God, you will say, if I do that my whole life will be ruined. How would I ever get on in the world? Herein lies the real place of Christian scholarship. Christian scholarship is the Church's prodigious invention to defend itself against the Bible, to ensure that we can continue to be good Christians without the Bible coming too close. Oh, priceless scholarship, what would we do without you? Dreadful it is to fall into the hands of the living God. Yes it is even dreadful to be alone with the New Testament. (Soren Kierkegaard)

We can only do the works of Christ if we have the love of Christ. Jesus says in Matthew 22:37-40 to

"Love the Lord your God with all your heart and with all your soul and with all your mind." This is the first and greatest commandment. And the second is like it: "Love your neighbor as yourself." All the Law and the Prophets hang on these two commandments.

It is possible to do the healings, miracles, and casting out of demons Jesus did without love. We are warned that even those who profess Jesus as Lord and drive out demons and heal the sick, are not necessarily going to be saved. We are supposed to be showing love by helping those in need.

Then the King will turn to those on the left and say, "Away with you, you cursed ones, into the eternal fire prepared for the Devil and his demons! For I was hungry, and you didn't feed me. I was thirsty, and you didn't give me anything to drink. I was a stranger, and you didn't invite me into your home. I was naked, and you gave me no clothing. I was sick and in prison, and you didn't visit me." Then they will reply, "Lord, when did we ever see you hungry or thirsty or a stranger or naked or sick or in prison, and not help you?" And he will answer, " I assure you, when you refused to help the least of these my brothers and sisters, you were refusing to help me." And they will go away into eternal punishment, but the righteous will go into eternal life. (Matthew 25:41-46 NLT)

How do we know if someone is a Christian? The LORD says we will know them by their love. He also describes the qualities and fruit of the Spirit in several places. Second Peter 2:5-11 reads:

For this very reason, make every effort to add to your faith goodness; and to goodness, knowledge; and to knowledge, self-control; and to self-control, perseverance; and to perseverance, godliness; and to godliness, brotherly kindness; and to brotherly kindness, love. For if you possess these qualities in increasing measure, they will keep you from being ineffective and unproductive in your knowledge of our Lord Jesus Christ. But if anyone does not have them, he is nearsighted and blind, and has forgotten that he has been cleansed from his past sins. Therefore, my brothers, be all the more eager to make your calling and election sure. For if you do these things, you will never fall, and you will receive a rich welcome into the eternal kingdom of our Lord and Savior Jesus Christ.

We are admonished to **do** something here. We are to "make every effort" to produce these qualities in ourselves that will keep us "from being ineffective and unproductive" in our knowledge of Jesus. We're also told to "make our calling and election sure." There is action that we need to take.

Then the eleven disciples went to Galilee, to the mountain where Jesus had told them to go. When they saw him, they worshiped him; but some doubted. Then Jesus came to them and said, "All authority in heaven and on earth has been given to me. Therefore go and make disciples of all nations, baptizing them in the name of the Father and of the Son and of the Holy Spirit, and teaching them to obey everything I have commanded you. And surely I am with you always, to the very end of the age." (Matthew 28:16-20 TNIV)

We are not to just tell people about Jesus, but "teach" them to obey Jesus. This is something we as a church tend to neglect. It's not good enough to have faith in Jesus, we have to have a faith that is followed by works.

What good is it, my brothers and sisters, if people claim to have faith but have no deeds? Can such faith save them? Suppose a brother or sister is without clothes and daily food. If one of you says to them, "Go in peace; keep warm and well fed," but does nothing about their physical needs, what good is it? In the same way, faith by itself, if it is not accompanied by action, is dead. But someone will say, "You have faith; I have deeds." Show me your faith without deeds, and I will show you my faith by what I do. You believe that there is one God. Good! Even the demons believe that—and shudder.

You foolish person, do you want evidence that faith without deeds is useless? Was not our father Abraham considered righteous for what he did when he offered his son Isaac on the altar? You see that his faith and his actions were working together, and his faith was made complete by what he did. And the scripture was fulfilled that says, "Abraham believed God, and it was credited to him as righteousness," and he was called God's friend. You see that people are justified by what they do and not by faith alone.

In the same way, was not even Rahab the prostitute considered righteous for what she did when she gave lodging to the spies and sent them off in a different direction? As the body without the spirit is dead, so faith without deeds is dead. (James 2:14-26)

Who are we fooling with our "religion"? Do we really have as firm a foundation as we think? What is our foundation? Is it the words of men or is all our hope and faith leaning on the solid rock, which is Christ the LORD? If we cannot read through the New Testament without trying to fit it into our theology or modifying it to fit our lifestyle or the belief system that has been handed down to us, maybe it's time to examine what our foundation really is. Even if we have the possibility of being saved "as one escaping through the flames", is that a solid foundation? Are you willing to risk eternity on this foundation?

James pleads with believers to be doers of the word and not just hearers.

But be doers of the word, and not hearers only, deceiving yourselves. For if anyone is a hearer of the word and not a doer, he is like a man observing his natural face in a mirror; for he observes himself, goes away, and immediately forgets what kind of man he was. But he who looks into the perfect law of liberty and continues in it, and is not a forgetful hearer but a doer of the work, this one will be blessed in what he does. (James 1:22-25 NKJV)

James says that we deceive ourselves when we are not obedient. Paul and Barnabas also hit on this theme throughout the book of Acts. *"So the word of God spread. The number of disciples in Jerusalem increased rapidly, and a large number of priests became obedient to the faith"* (Acts 6:7). This passage says the priests became obedient. There is obviously an outward manifestation of an inward change of heart.

They [Paul & Barnabas] *preached the good news in that city and won a large number of disciples. Then they returned to Lystra, Iconium and Antioch, strengthening the disciples and encouraging them to remain true to the faith. "We must go through many hardships to enter the kingdom of God," they said.* (Acts 14:21-22)

Paul and Barnabas encourage the disciples to "remain true to the faith" and remind them that they "must go through many hardships to enter the kingdom of God." This indicates something that we have to do. It does not mean that we add to the finished work of Jesus. We need to be clear on that, but it does mean that there are works "prepared in advance" that we need to be doing. The Bible even indicates that we are rewarded for the good works done in faith.

By the grace God has given me, I laid a foundation as a wise builder, and someone else is building on it. But each one should build with care. For no one can lay any foundation other than the one already laid, which is Jesus Christ. If anyone builds on this foundation using gold, silver, costly stones, wood, hay or straw, their work will be shown for what it is, because the

Day will bring it to light. It will be revealed with fire, and the fire will test the quality of each person's work. If what has been built survives, the builder will receive a reward. If it is burned up, the builder will suffer loss but yet will be saved—even though only as one escaping through the flames.
(1 Corinthians 3:10-15)

We build on the foundation of Jesus Christ. Our works will be tested and shown for what they really are. Our faith will produce works, and they need to be righteous works. Revelation chapters two and three speak to the idea that faith produces works. Christ is speaking to the angels of the churches. He is saying to the angels of the churches that He knows the churches' "works or deeds". He is not saying "I know your hearts" and am therefore either pleased or not.

So, does saying Christ is LORD save you or your church and guarantee entrance into heaven? Perhaps a few more verses are needed. Here is a letter to Titus from Paul. He is instructing Titus on what his job is in Crete. Verse 16 is especially interesting with regard to this church and people, as it should be to us. We can claim to know God all we want, but it appears our actions must line up as well.

The reason I left you in Crete was that you might straighten out what was left unfinished and appoint elders in every town, as I directed you. An elder must be blameless, the husband of but one wife, a man whose children believe and are not open to the charge of being wild and disobedient. Since an overseer is entrusted with God's work, he must be blameless—not overbearing, not quick-tempered, not given to drunkenness, not violent, not pursuing dishonest gain. Rather he must be hospitable, one who loves what is good, who is self-controlled, upright, holy and disciplined. He must hold firmly to the trustworthy message as it has been taught, so that he can encourage others by sound doctrine and refute those who oppose it.

For there are many rebellious people, mere talkers and deceivers, especially those of the circumcision group. They must be silenced, because they are ruining whole households by teaching things they ought not to teach—and that for the sake of dishonest gain. Even one of their own prophets has said, "Cretans are always liars, evil brutes, lazy gluttons." This testimony is true. Therefore, rebuke them sharply, so that they will be sound in the faith and will pay no attention to Jewish myths or to the commands of those who reject the truth. To the pure, all things are pure, but to those who are corrupted and do not believe, nothing is pure. In fact, both their minds and consciences are corrupted. They claim to know God, but by their actions they deny him. They are detestable, disobedient and unfit for doing anything good. (Titus 1:5-16)

What do these verses and diatribe against the Cretans and Jewish myths have to do with the church today? Again, everything we believe must be filtered through the Word. Paul was dealing with a group of people here who were getting away from the simple truth of salvation through Christ. People were being deceived, and believing they needed to perform rituals and other things that do not produce fruit. Our walk, our talk, and our deeds must produce fruit! Love, joy, peace, patience, kindness, goodness, faithfulness, gentleness and self control is the fruit of the Spirit (Galatians 5:22-23). These are the things that, when tested by the by the fire of God will stand. These are the solid building blocks that are not made of wood or straw.

We really need to discern through the Holy Spirit what is of God and what is not. *"And no wonder! For Satan himself transforms himself into an angel of light. Therefore it is no great thing if his ministers also transform themselves into ministers of righteousness, whose end will be according to their works"* (2 Corinthians 11:14-15 NKJV). It is the works that will determine what happens to these people who profess Jesus as Lord, but don't really mean it with their lives. They're actually ministers of the devil.

70

We need to make sure we are ministers of God and not the evil one. We are admonished to examine ourselves *"as to whether you are in the faith. Test yourselves. Do you not know yourselves, that Jesus Christ is in you?-unless indeed you are disqualified"* (2 Corinthians 13:5 NKJV). The word "examine" in this verse is peirazo, Strong's #3985. It means "to explore, test, try, assay, examine, prove, attempt, tempt. The word describes the testing of the believer's loyalty, strength, opinions, disposition, condition, faith, patience, or character. Peirazo determines which way one is going and what one is made of." (NKJV New Spirit Filled Life Bible, p. 1820) This is the same word that Jesus uses in Revelation chapter two when He tells the church in Smyrna some of them are going to be thrown into prison in order to peirazo them.

Does it take faith alone? Yes, but as we see, faith is more than a mental assent to some truth, but is instead a life-changing obedience and fully persuaded heart regarding the promises of God. The saved will show their faith by what they do. Faith tested by purifying fire will come through brilliant, and strong, and the works will be lasting to the glory of God.

In other words, a Christian will produce good fruit. Here is what Strong's has to say about the original Greek word for fruit and it's meaning.

Strong's G2590 Karpos

1) **fruit**
   a) the fruit of the trees, vines, of the fields
   b) the fruit of one's loins, i.e. his progeny, his posterity

2) **that which originates or comes from something, an effect, result**
   a) work, act, deed
   b) advantage, profit, utility
   c) praises, which are presented to God as a thank offering

d) to gather fruit (i.e. a reaped harvest) into life eternal (as into a granary), is used in fig. discourse of those who by their labours have fitted souls to obtain eternal life

So, what kinds of fruit are listed in the Word? There is good fruit and there is bad fruit. John the Baptist preached that *"every tree that does not produce good fruit will be chopped down and thrown into the fire"* (Matthew 3:10, NLT). Let's define good and bad fruit.

Bitter fruit is the result of living our own way. Those who ignore God's calling, and His reaching out to them, rejecting His advice and who hate knowledge – these are the ones God says He will laugh, mock and, not answer, as calamity, disaster, anguish, distress, and finally death overtakes them. (Proverbs 1)

Fools, (complacent) simpletons (turn away) and mockers (mock) are the three kinds of people who are addressed here in Proverbs 1. It seems that in God's view there is simply no excuse for not following Him. He leaves no doubt about that. We know that God is love. However, Proverbs 1 almost has the tone of God taking revenge on those who generate "bitter fruit" or at least comforting those whose lives have been impacted by those negatively described here. Proverbs 1:31 is especially pointed for those who reject Him! "They must eat the bitter fruit of living their own way, choking on their own schemes." Would anyone in their right mind want to be on this side of an omnipotent God?

Fruitless deeds of darkness are mentioned in Ephesians 5:11. This stands in contrast to other places where God, in the Bible, talks about sinful or evil fruit. Paul is saying that the deeds of darkness will bear no fruit toward eternal life in God's Kingdom. Further, he says that these deeds should be exposed by those who are living in the light. Are we supposed to judge people then? Well, if we'll know true Christ followers by their fruit, we'll have to judge whether the fruit they bear is "good" or "bad" fruit, right?

Paul is saying that we are supposed to expose the fruitless deeds of darkness. A judgment as to whether deeds (fruit) are good or bad will be required to do this. A mentality of "well I can't say if that's good or bad" is not what is being promoted here. We should of course never pass a sentence of heaven or hell on someone as only God can possibly know that for sure. We should, however be prepared to confront someone who bears bad or no fruit with the truth of the Word.

Bad fruit is the opposite of good fruit. As you read Matthew 7:15-23 the words of verse 21 should be especially chilling: *"Not everyone who says to Me, 'Lord, Lord,' will enter the kingdom of heaven."* Wow, so what does that mean anyway? Well, the second half of the verse contains the answer. *"[B]ut **he who does the will of My Father who is in heaven will enter.**"* The verses preceding this speak to fruit, good or bad. However, even those who are bearing good fruit may not be saved if the fruit they are bearing is not the will of the Father. Some examples of this are: doing religion, performing tradition, and other activities not called for by God. Examples of this are given in Isaiah 66:1-5, where God has given the Israelites the law and tells them how He wants to be worshiped, However, they have turned these into simple acts of tradition and religion and have forgotten to listen to God and to do the things He tells them.

Maybe what to us appears to be good fruit really is not then? We must constantly test our motives and test whether the LORD has actually called us to do what we're doing. Our tendency is to do over and over what makes us feel spiritual, or possibly doing that thing which caused us to feel close to God at some prior time in our lives. Have you noticed that God seems to like uniqueness and change? Just look at snowflakes or mountains, flowers, people . . . and on and on. They are all different. The LORD says several times, "Sing unto Me a **new** song."

We really need to be hearing God to know that the fruit we are producing is good fruit. That is the bottom line. Will you follow someone you believe is hearing God (even a pastor), and trust your eternal destiny to them? (Think of Jim Jones, or David Koresh or Marshall Applewhite here.) How can you know that you are doing exactly what God wants you to do, unless you are in communion with Him? You need to be hearing from God yourself.

Fruit for death. (Romans 7:4-6 NIV) The Israelites appeared to be tied down by the law, they didn't seem to have a real desire to obey God out of love, but instead the law was kind of like a leash that restrained them. So they always desired to be disobedient, and God kept them in check with the law. What God really always wanted was for Him to be their God and for them to be His people. Then Paul goes on to say that the law isn't sin either, for without it how could we know the mind of God regarding our thinking and actions, or what He considers right and wrong? But now the law of the Spirit supersedes the written code. If we live according to the Spirit our minds are set on what the Spirit desires instead of worldly desires. Our sinful nature is aroused by the law because without the Holy Spirit to guide us we naturally gravitate toward sin. We try to somehow look better because "we" obey the law, where others don't do as well. Or we try to circumvent the law, because of our sinful nature.

Good fruit. Good fruit is what is produced when we are in Christ Jesus. This is what the will (Matt. 7:21) of the Father is. John 6:40 says, *"For my Father's will is that everyone who looks to the Son and believes in him shall have eternal life, and I will raise him up at the last day."* If we believe in the Son how could we produce anything but good fruit? The Holy Spirit living in us leads us toward righteousness and conformity to the image of Christ. (Romans 8:29) It is when we look at ourselves that we start to produce bad fruit. Self-centeredness leads to pride, and all kinds of sin.

So what exactly is "Good Fruit" then? And how will we know it? Well, notice what Matthew 7:22 says, these people who Jesus says He never knew, are telling him what they had done. Their works! They are not saying they love Him, they just think they deserve to enter the kingdom of heaven based on their works. He says He never knew them - and rightly so it seems. He says, *"depart from Me you who practice lawlessness."* If we are counting on works or the law to save us, we can never achieve the holiness required to be saved and would then be viewed as lawless people. In fact we are dependent on grace. The only way we can be viewed as holy in the sight of God is if He views us through the lens of His Son, so that when He looks at us, He sees His Son and not our shortcomings. So then, good fruit is what is produced in our lives when we are in Christ. We know it is good fruit when it is done to His glory and for no other purpose. God knows our motives. Are our motives pure? Are we doing things for any reason other than Christ, or are we looking for personal gain (popularity, money, recognition, power, etc.) Or, are we doing things simply out of love for our LORD and Savior?

Either you are a tree producing good fruit or a tree producing bad fruit. It is through faith in Jesus' finished work that we will produce any good fruit.

> [1]*"I am the true vine, and my Father is the gardener. [2]He cuts off every branch in me that bears no fruit, while every branch that does bear fruit he prunes[a] so that it will be even more fruitful. [3]You are already clean because of the word I have spoken to you. [4]Remain in me, and I will remain in you. No branch can bear fruit by itself; it must remain in the vine. Neither can you bear fruit unless you remain in me.*

> [5]*"I am the vine; you are the branches. If a man remains in me and I in him, he will bear much fruit; apart from me you can do nothing. [6]If anyone does not remain in me, he is like a branch that is thrown away and withers; such branches are picked up, thrown into the fire and burned. [7]If you remain in me and my words remain in you, ask whatever you wish, and it will be given you. [8]This is to my Father's glory, that you bear much fruit, showing yourselves to be my disciples.*

Fruit to God. This fruit (Romans 7:4) is what is born when we have died to the Law and for us to live is Christ. We now serve the new way of the Spirit and not the written code. We produce fruit to God through faith.

Proverbs 11:30 reads, *"The fruit of the righteous is a tree of life, and he who wins souls is wise."*

Fruit of the Spirit. (Galatians 5:22) The fruit of the Spirit is love, joy, peace, patience, kindness, goodness, faithfulness, gentleness, and self-control. This verse can be used as a kind of guide to see if your motives are pure. But using this shouldn't be the only test. We tend to be so deceitful, that we can rationalize anything and twist these words to fit a desired outcome. We really need to know the heart of God and listen to what He is telling us. The Spirit of truth will lead us into all truth. Our own intellect will not get us there.

Fruits of labor are a gift from God. We should enjoy these fruits! (Ecclesiastes 3:13)

Fruit of our lips. This is the sacrifice of praise, which we should always be lifting up to God. (Hebrews 13:15)

God is very patient with us and desires us to bear good fruit (Luke 13:1-8). He shows us how to bear good fruit and gives us His very Son as an example for us to follow. Then He empowers us with the Spirit of Christ to help us to defeat the desire to bear bad fruit. He tells us if we are in Christ we will bear good fruit! What a comfort! If we are not bearing good fruit we must try to change this. His patience doesn't last forever. (Luke 13:9) At some point we will be judged according to our fruit. (Matt. 7:21, Proverbs 1, John 15:1-2, Luke 13:6-8)

It is faith that will produce the fruit of righteousness, the good fruit, that pleases God. Our faith needs to be obedient faith in order to produce the good fruit.

CHAPTER 9

What Do You Mean Limited Atonement?

O
ne of the reasons for writing this book is that many people have
been deceived by a theology that says God creates some people
for hell and some people for heaven. This kind of teaching goes directly
against the purpose of creation laid out in the Bible. This theology is
a teaching of man, and we do not follow man, but God. For we do not
follow any man, but Christ alone. Christ is not divided (1 Cor. 1:13), and
it is our hope in writing this, that His people will no longer be divided,
but come together in unity and in Truth. We do not intend to slander a
man long since dead, but we do intend to refute anything that is not truth.
There are bits of truth in various theologies, but it is not Truth itself.

A new Christian reading the Bible for the first time would never come up
with the idea that Jesus only came to save a few, or that the atonement of
Jesus Christ is in any way limited. We have to be taught by men to believe
in limited atonement. The Bible clearly states that God wants everyone to
be saved (see chapters 1 & 2). Also the Bible states that we must accept
the gift of salvation through faith in Christ (John 6:40). It's simple.

There are many arguments for the limited atonement of Jesus Christ. We desire to show you in this chapter that those arguments do not match what Scripture says.

Some people arguing for limited atonement use Romans 8:28-30.

And we know that in all things God works for the good of those who love him, who have been called according to his purpose. For those God foreknew he also predestined to be conformed to the likeness of his Son, that he might be the firstborn among many brothers. And those he predestined, he also called; those he called, he also justified; those he justified, he also glorified.

We have already discussed that God did predestine those he foreknew. God foreknew, or knew beforehand, who would choose life. This is different from deciding for them what will happen.

Limited atonement proponents also use Acts 13:48 to defend their view, which states: *"When the Gentiles heard this, they were glad and honored the word of the Lord; and all who were appointed for eternal life believed."* Those who believe in limited atonement propose that since the Bible says the Gentiles mentioned in the previous statement were "appointed," then it is clear that God wants to save some and not save others. This is a good argument for limited atonement if it is taken as a scripture by itself, but it definitely does not hold up to the rest of scripture that tells how God wants all people to be saved. (See chapter two.) "Appointed" is the same as "predestined." We know that God predestined those he <u>foreknew</u>. God knows who will believe and who will not. Therefore, this argument just does not have any merit.

John 3:16-18 reads,

For God so loved the world that he gave his one and only Son, that whoever believes in him shall not perish but have eternal life. For

God did not send his Son into the world to condemn the world, but to save the world through him. Whoever believes in him is not condemned, but whoever does not believe stands condemned already because he has not believed in the name of God's one and only Son.

The unbelievers in the above passage are not condemned because of some choice God made on their behalf before even creating them, but they stand condemned "already" because they did not believe. God knows those who will choose life, but He still allows them that choice.

Additionally, the story of Jacob and Esau tends to be used as an argument for predestination. God did choose Jacob, but we see in the twins' lives that Esau despised what God gave him and Jacob wrestled with God until he got a blessing. Jacob was a liar and a thief, but God blessed him because he wanted God so badly, he wouldn't quit pursuing Him. The Lord loves that.

Romans 9:13 says, *"Jacob I have loved, but Esau I have hated."* On the surface, it certainly looks like God predestined Jacob and Esau for heaven and hell. However, going deeper in the Word will show that this isn't the case.

The first statement is on the very surface. The next layer we need to look at is the full statement from Romans 9:13 *"As it is written, 'Jacob I have loved, but Esau I have hated.'"* We first need to know where the *"as it is written"* part comes from. There is a footnote in the New King James Version telling us where this verse comes from, which is Genesis 25:23 (NKJV)

And the LORD said to her:
"Two nations are in your womb,
Two peoples shall be separated from your body;
One people shall be stronger than the other,

And the older shall serve the younger."

Rebekah inquired of the LORD regarding the struggle which was going on inside of her. God answered her with the above words. God is clearly speaking to Jacob and Esau as nations, and not as individuals. God is speaking of those nations that would come from her womb, which are Israel (Jacob) and Edom (Esau). God's word came to fulfillment in 1 Chronicles when the Edomites became subject to Israel.

1 Chronicles 18:13 (NKJV) says, *"He also put garrisons in Edom, and all the Edomites became David's servants. And the LORD preserved David wherever he went."*

The next footnote listed regarding Romans 9:13 is Malachi 1:2-5, which reads:

> "I have always loved you," says the Lord.
> But you retort, "Really? How have you loved us?"
> And the Lord replies, "This is how I showed my love for you: I loved your ancestor Jacob, but I rejected his brother, Esau, and devastated his hill country. I turned Esau's inheritance into a desert for jackals."
> Esau's descendants in Edom may say, "We have been shattered, but we will rebuild the ruins."
>
> But the Lord of Heaven's Armies replies, "They may try to rebuild, but I will demolish them again. Their country will be known as 'The Land of Wickedness,' and their people will be called 'The People with Whom the Lord Is Forever Angry.' When you see the destruction for yourselves, you will say, 'Truly, the Lord's greatness reaches far beyond Israel's borders!'" (NLT)

Truly, God hates wickedness and we see that truth in verse 4 of Malachi 1. Edom was wicked. God did not cause or author the wickedness of

Edom any more than He authored it in us. Can God be the author of evil? Where would He get something which He is not? Isn't our LORD perfect in all His ways? He is the very definition of love, justice, mercy and of course sovereignty. God does not need to cause everything to happen in order for Him to be sovereign. Man's limited sovereignty (free will) doesn't threaten Him. He maintains control in spite of this. There is one who is the author of all manner of evil though, and his name is Satan. By his very nature, he cannot do anything except evil. He is called the Father of Lies and we are told that lying is natural to him. When a people or nation follow the devil instead of the Lord, they are rejecting that which can save them.

So can the argument of predestination still stand since God did predestine these two nations? Well, consider, do all Israelites go to heaven? Or, do all descendants of Esau go to hell? Of course not. Jesus died to save all who have or will call on His name. The new covenant encompasses the Gentiles too, and that includes Edom. This truth is written of in Romans 10:11-13.

> *For the Scripture says,* "Whoever believes on Him will not be put to shame." *For there is no distinction between Jew and Greek, for the same Lord over all is rich to all who call upon Him. For* "whoever calls on the name of the LORD shall be saved."

Speaking of Jacob, Hosea 12:3-5 reads,

> He took his brother by the heel in the womb,
> And in his strength he struggled with God.
> Yes, he struggled with the Angel and prevailed.
> He wept, and sought favor from Him.
> He found Him in Bethel,
> And there He spoke to us –
> That is, the LORD God of hosts.
> The LORD is His memorable name. (NKJV)

Second Corinthians 4:4 says, *"The god of this age has blinded the minds of unbelievers, so that they cannot see the light of the gospel that displays the glory of Christ, who is the image of God.* The word "blinded" means hardened, as when we constantly resist and so become dull to the power of understanding. Additionally, the blinding is done by the god of this age, who is Satan. It is the same idea portrayed in Romans 11:7, which states, *"What then? Israel hath not obtained that which he seeketh for; but the election hath obtained it and the rest were blinded" (KJV).* The blinding spoken of is the fault of the unbeliever. There is no excuse.

The reason Paul wrote the above verse in Romans is to clarify what he wrote a few verses before, which is also used to as an argument against the full atonement of Jesus Christ. Romans 11:5-10 (NKJV) reads:

> *Even so then, at this present time there is a remnant according to the election of grace. And if by grace, then it is no longer of works; otherwise grace is no longer grace. But if it is of works, it is no longer grace; otherwise work is no longer work. What then? Israel has not obtained what it seeks; but the elect have obtained it, and the rest were blinded. Just as it is written:*
> > *'God has given them a spirit of stupor,*
> > *Eyes that they should not see*
> > *And ears that they should not hear,*
> > *To this very day.'*
> *And David says:*
> > *'Let their table become a snare and a trap,*
> > *A stumbling block and a recompense to them.*
> > *Let their eyes be darkened, so that they do not see,*
> > *And bow down their back always.'*

Reading this passage alone, outside of the rest of scripture sure would make it seem like God makes some people so they can understand and some so that they cannot just so some will be saved and some will not. However, in the light of the rest of the Word, we can see that is not at all what God is saying. Just a few verses later He says, *"Because of unbelief they were broken off, and you stand by faith. Do not be haughty, but fear"* (Romans 11:20). So, we see that it was because of persistent unbelief that their hearts were hardened. This unbelief as a hindrance to salvation and understanding of the Kingdom of God is the same thing Jesus spoke of when He said:

> *In them is fulfilled the prophecy of Isaiah:*
>   *'You will be ever hearing but never understanding;*
>   *you will be ever seeing but never perceiving.*
>   *For this people's heart has become calloused;*
>   *they hardly hear with their ears,*
>   *and they have closed their eyes.*
>   *Otherwise they might see with their eyes,*
>   *hear with their ears,*
>   *understand with their hearts*
>   *and turn, and I would heal them.*

Here Jesus is talking about those people who did not understand His parables. Only those who really sought to understand what they meant, were told the meaning of the parables. Those who heard, but did not really want to know Jesus or what He was saying to them, hardened their hearts so that even though He spoke, they could not "hear" Him. Even though they saw miracles, they did not "see" them because of persistent unbelief. Those who grew in the grace and knowledge of Jesus Christ are those who applied themselves to understand and were persistent in their pursuit of the One True God.

Someone asked Jesus as He was going to Jerusalem, *"Lord, are only a few people going to be saved?" Jesus responded:*

> *Make every effort to enter through the narrow door, because many, I tell you, will try to enter and will not be able to. Once the owner*

of the house gets up and closes the door, you will stand outside knocking, and pleading, "Sir, open the door for us."
But he will answer, "I don't know you or where you come from."
Then you will say, "We ate and drank with you, and you taught in our streets."
But he will reply, "I don't know you or where you come from. Away from me, all you evildoers!"
There will be weeping there, and gnashing of teeth, when you see Abraham, Isaac, and Jacob and all the prophets in the kingdom of God, but you yourselves thrown out. People will come from east and west and north and south, and will take their places at the feast in the kingdom of God. Indeed there are those who are last who will be first, and first who will be last.
Luke 13:23-30

Jesus tells us to make every effort to enter through the narrow door. This effort would not be necessary if we didn't have some sort of choice in choosing salvation or rejecting it. The other lesson to be noted here is that the people knocking on the door thought they were saved, and they were not. We cannot depend on a theology to save us or a mental assertion that Jesus is Lord. We must have that revelation in our hearts and live with Jesus really being Lord of our lives. Why did Jesus Christ come? So that we *"may know Him who is true"* (1 John 5:20).

When we perceive who Jesus is, it is a revelation from God, but it can definitely come from our desire to perceive who He is.

The following are several verses used by those who believe that only God initiates salvation and that God creates some people for the purpose of eternity in hell and some people for eternity in heaven. With this particular theology a person only chooses to believe because they really have no choice – it's been chosen for them and they're just going along with it.

- **John 6:37** *All that the Father gives to me will come to me, and whoever comes to me I will never drive away.*

- **John 6:44** *No one can come to me unless the Father who sent me draws him, and I will raise him up at the last day.*

- **John 6:65** *He went on to say, "This is why I told you that no one can come to me unless the Father has enabled him."*

Taken alone, these verses would indicate the argument stated above. However, taken with the rest of scripture, that is not the case. Let's look at 2 Corinthians 3:7-18 (NLT).

The old way, with laws etched in stone, led to death, though it began with such glory that the people of Israel could not bear to look at Moses' face. For his face shone with the glory of God, even though the brightness was already fading away. Shouldn't we expect far greater glory under the new way, now that the Holy Spirit is giving life? If the old way, which brings condemnation, was glorious, how much more glorious is the new way, which makes us right with God! In fact, that first glory was not glorious at all compared with the overwhelming glory of the new way. So if the old way, which has been replaced, was glorious, how much more glorious is the new, which remains forever!

*Since this new way gives us such confidence, we can be very bold. We are not like Moses, who put a veil over his face so the people of Israel would not see the glory, even though it was destined to fade away. But the people's minds were hardened, and to this day whenever the old covenant is being read, the same veil covers their minds so they cannot understand the truth. **And this veil can be removed only by believing in Christ.** Yes, even today when they read Moses' writings, their hearts are covered with that veil, and they do not understand.*

*But **whenever someone turns to the Lord, the veil is taken away**. For the Lord is the Spirit, and wherever the Spirit of the Lord is, there is freedom. So all of us who have had that veil removed can see and reflect the glory of the Lord. And the Lord – who is the Spirit – makes us more and more like him as we are changed into his glorious image.*

The veil is taken away when someone believes. It is not taken away before they believe so that they can believe. When Jesus performed a healing or a miracle for someone, others in the crowd responded. They decided that what Jesus had to offer was something they wanted too. There is no doubt that God can operate in any way He chooses. It is possible for Him to reveal Himself to someone who is really not seeking Truth, as in the case of the Apostle Paul. Paul was happy to persecute the followers of the Way. He was not seeking Truth. In that case, the Lord drew Paul to Himself and Paul responded. However, it is also possible that we initiate the drawing to Christ. John 6:37 above says that God will not drive us away if we come to Him. We are able to choose because God didn't make a bunch of robots that do whatever He programs them to do. That would mean that we could never really love Him. No, the Lord made people with freewill, so that they could choose to love Him. Without a choice to love, it's not really love.

We also see as we look at the rest of scripture in interpreting the verses listed above, that God draws all people to Himself. *"But I, when I am lifted up from the earth, will draw all men to myself"* (John 12:32). And Hebrews 10:32 states that we can "draw near to God." Additionally, He tells us that we are without excuse simply because of nature (Romans 1:20). We ought to be able to look around us and be able to see that there is a God, and because of the desire we all have to worship, we should be seeking that God that created us. So, in John 6:44, we are all drawn to God in some way or another. But, only those of us who really want Him will respond to that drawing by giving our lives to Jesus and making Him the Lord of our lives.

Some other verses used to promote limited atonement are Ephesians 1:4-6, 11 and 1 Thessalonians 1:4-5. These verses speak of being chosen and elected. We know the Bible will not contradict itself and Romans 8 tells us we are chosen because of foreknowledge. The word "predestined" also does not mean that some are excluded and some included, but shows that God has a plan for each one of us (Jeremiah 29:11).

Second Thessalonians 2:13 reads, *"But we ought always to thank God for you, brothers loved by the Lord, because from the beginning God chose you to be saved through the sanctifying work of the Spirit and through belief in the truth."* We are definitely chosen for salvation through Jesus if we believe. We have to believe. Jesus died for the sins of the world. We're all chosen for salvation if we will just believe.

Jesus spoke in Luke,

> *O Jerusalem, Jerusalem, you who kill the prophets and stone those sent to you, how often I have longed to gather your children together, as a hen gathers her chicks under her wings, but you were not willing! Look, your house is left to you desolate. I tell you, you will not see me again until you say, "Blessed is he who comes in the name of the Lord."* (13:34-35)

Jesus longs for the salvation of Jerusalem, but they refuse him. He does not force them to choose Him, even though He desires that they choose salvation through Him.

It's important to study the original language to get a better understanding of God's Word. First Timothy 5:21 says, *"I charge you, in the sight of God and Christ Jesus and the elect angels, to keep these instructions without partiality, and to do nothing out of favoritism."* Here some people believe that some angels are "elect" in the same sense they believe people are, unless they understand the meaning of the word "elect." Strong's #1588: The word designates one picked out from among the larger group for special services or privileges. It describes Christ as the chosen Messiah of God (Luke 23:35), angels as messengers from heaven (1 Tim 5:21), and believers as recipients of God's favor (Matt. 24:22; Rom 8:33; Col. 3:12). In other words, some angels have one job and some another. So, the argument for election here doesn't hold up either.

The theory of limited atonement is also argued for using 2 Timothy 1:9 and 1 Peter 1:1-2 and 2:9. Again, these verses speak of being chosen. We are chosen because we are believers. This makes us a royal priesthood, holy nation, etc. as the passage in 1 Peter goes on to say. We are elect because of foreknowledge. We are special as children of God, but we have to choose that life of faith in Christ. We're all given faith to believe. Christ tells us we only need faith the size of a mustard seed to move mountains. It's unbelief that stops that faith from moving, and unbelief that stops people from entering the Kingdom of Heaven.

We need to be sure we are not teaching others to have unbelief, but instead, we need to be encouraging and building each other up in faith. May it not be said of us: *"Woe to you lawyers! For you have taken away the key of knowledge. You did not enter in yourselves, and those who were entering in you hindered."* (Luke 11:52 NKJV)

God is love. When we really believe that, we know that God does not create people for the sole purpose of sending them to hell. We know that God loves everything He created because that's what the Word says, and the Word is truth.

You have heard that it was said, "Love your neighbor and hate your enemy." But I tell you: Love your enemies and pray for those who persecute you, that you may be sons of your Father in heaven. He causes his sun to rise on the evil and the good, and sends rain on the righteous and the unrighteous. If you love those who love you, what reward will you get? Are not even the tax collectors doing that? And if you greet only your brothers, what are you doing more than others? Do not even pagans do that? Be perfect, therefore, as your heavenly Father is perfect. (Matthew 5:43-48)

When God tells us that we are to love everyone, we can be sure it is because He is doing the same thing. He loves everyone. If even the pagans love those who love them, the Lord would be no better than a pagan if all He did was love those who love Him. Because God so loved the world, He gave Jesus Christ. That's the truth. That's good theology. We do not follow man, but Jesus Christ. Paul addresses this in one of his letters to the Corinthians.

". . .One of you says, 'I follow Paul'; another, 'I follow Apollos'; another, 'I follow Cephas'; still another, 'I follow Christ.' Is Christ divided? Was Paul crucified for you? Were you baptized into the name of Paul?" (1 Corinthians 1:12-13)

Try putting your favorite theologian's name in for Paul's and see how the above verse reads. No man, except Christ, died for you. No one can save you, except Christ. Jesus Christ is perfect theology. Follow Him.

CHAPTER 10

Authority

And Jesus came and spoke to them, saying, "All authority has been given to Me in heaven and on earth. Go therefore and make disciples of all the nations, baptizing them in the name of the Father, and of the Son, and of the Holy Spirit, teaching them to observe all things that I have commanded you; and lo, I am with you always, even to the end of the age."
Matthew 28:18-20 NKJV

Jesus is not speaking as God in the above verses. Jesus was given authority, which means it was taken from someone. That someone is our enemy, the devil. Everything in the spiritual realm operates according to authority. Demons are only driven out because of the authority Jesus has over them. It is imperative that believers know their authority in order to do battle in the heavenly realms according to Ephesians chapter six. The concept of authority is important to understand in order to understand the fullness of what Jesus has done for us on the cross.

Let's go back to the beginning of creation. God placed Adam and Eve in the garden and told them to subdue it and rule over it. Adam actually named every animal, which just goes to show how far we have fallen.

Adam was able to name and remember all the animals. We certainly can't do that today. Scientists say we use only a fraction of our brains. Sin has definitely wreaked havoc in mankind.

So, we see that Adam, along with Eve, was given authority over the earth. God created man and gave him authority in the earth. He says that *"The heaven, even the heavens, are the LORD's; But the earth He has given to the children of men."* (Psalm 115:16 NKJV) So what happened to our authority? Authority cannot be stripped away, but it can definitely be given away, and that is exactly what happened on earth.

When Adam and Eve decided to trust the devil, and disobey God, they gave up their authority on earth to the devil. That is why Jesus calls Satan the prince of this world. Ephesians 2:2 (NKJV) reads, *". . . in which you once walked according to the course of this world, according to <u>the prince of the power of the air</u>, the spirit who now works in the sons of disobedience . . .".* Jesus also calls Satan the ruler of this world in John 14:30 when He says, *"I will no longer talk much with you, for the ruler of this world is coming, and he has nothing in Me."* Satan became the ruler of the world when Adam gave the devil his authority by submitting to sin. We are in bondage to sin when we sin, and if you are in bondage to something, it rules over you. That is why we have to *"put to death the misdeeds of the body"* (Romans 8:13), so we can live.

So, if Adam and Eve gave their authority to the devil, what can man do to get that authority back? It takes a miracle. It takes the resurrection of the perfect Man, Jesus Christ. In speaking of His death and resurrection, Jesus said, *"Now is the judgment of this world; now the ruler of this world will be cast out"* (John 12:31). And in speaking of the coming of the Holy Spirit, Jesus says that His Spirit will convict the world *"of judgment, because the ruler of this world is judged"* (John 16:11 NKJV).

"So it is written: 'The first man Adam became a living being'; the last Adam, a life-giving spirit." (1 Corinthians 15:45) The first Adam sinned

and death became the victor. The last Adam is Jesus. He did not sin, but mastered death, and now victory is in Jesus. First Corinthians 15:46 tells us that *"The spiritual did not come first, but the natural, and after that the spiritual."* Jesus is the fulfillment of all prophecy. The fact that God created Adam from dust and then breathed life into him is a prophecy to what would happen through Christ. Jesus breathes life into us when we are still sinners. He resurrects us from the dead because death has no power over us any longer. We are free, and we are empowered to bring His Kingdom to earth, just as He taught us to pray (see Matthew 6 and Luke 11).

The symbol of authority in the Bible is keys. The Lord wants you to understand how this relates to salvation and the fact that God loves the whole world. Read Isaiah 22:20-22 (NKJV). It says:

> *Then it shall be in that day,*
> *That I will call My servant . . .*
> *I will clothe him with your robe*
> *And strengthen him with your belt;*
> *I will commit your responsibility into his hand.*
> *He shall be a father to the inhabitants of Jerusalem*
> *And to the house of Judah.*
> *The key of the house of David*
> *I will lay on his shoulder;*
> *So he shall open, and no one shall shut;*
> *And he shall shut, and no one shall open.*

Many prophecies have several fulfillments, but they are all ultimately fulfilled in Jesus because Jesus is the Spirit of Prophecy. So, in the above passage, we need to see that Jesus is clothed in man's body (the *robe*). He has taken our sin (taken our *responsibility*). Because Jesus takes this responsibility, our sin, He is then given the *"key of the house of David."* With this key of authority, there are doors He will open that none can shut, and doors He will shut that none can open. No one can shut the way to heaven which Jesus has opened for us! Satan cannot open the door to authority which has been taken from him either, unless we give it to him. Giving Satan back the authority that Jesus died to take from him, is what gives Satan the right to oppress, make sick, torment, and torture people in earth and in hell.

It is established that Jesus took authority back from the devil, but how can we be sure that Jesus has given us the authority He took back? We can be sure because He tells us, and His Word never fails, for it is impossible for Him to lie. Matthew 16:19 (NKJV) reads, *"And I will give you the keys of the kingdom of heaven, and whatever you bind on earth will be bound in heaven, and whatever you loose on earth will be loosed in heaven."* And again in Matthew 18:18 (NKJV), Jesus reiterates what He said before: *"Assuredly, I say to you, whatever you bind on earth will be bound in heaven, and whatever you loose on earth will be loosed in heaven."* He is telling us that the keys are given back to us because of what He has done.

Matthew 16:18 is talking about building His Church upon the revelation of Jesus Christ by the Holy Spirit. This verse tells us that the power of hell will not conquer the Church. Jesus also says He will give the Church authority (keys), so we, being the Church, have power to bind and loose. In fact, we are a Royal Priesthood (1 Peter 2:9). Because we are royalty, we have power on earth, and because we are priests, we have spiritual authority. This authority is effective only by the Holy Spirit (grace). Whoever uses the authority from Jesus must use it while walking in the Spirit, and so it is effective only within realm of the will of God. Matthew 18:18 says the basic same thing about the authority of the Church.

A good, short book of the Bible to read for understanding regarding authority and the atonement is the book of Ephesians.

> *I keep asking that the God of our Lord Jesus Christ, the glorious Father, may give you the Spirit of wisdom and revelation, so*

that you may know him better. I pray also that the eyes of your heart may be enlightened in order that you may know the hope to which he has called you, the riches of his glorious inheritance in the saints, and his incomparably great power for us who believe. That power is like the working of his mighty strength, which he exerted in Christ when he raised him from the dead and seated him at his right hand in the heavenly realms, far above all rule and authority, power and dominion, and every title that can be given, not only in the present age but also in the one to come. And God placed all things under his feet and appointed him to be head over everything for the church, which is his body, the fullness of him who fills everything in every way.

***

And God raised us up with Christ and seated us with him in the heavenly realms in Christ Jesus,
Ephesians 1:17-23; Ephesians 2:6

From these verses, we can see that Jesus is above all other authority. There is nothing above Him. What He did through His sacrifice was enough. To add to the wonder of it all, we can see that through the atonement of Jesus, we too are seated in the heavenly realms with all things under our feet. This is why it says: *"When he ascended on high, he led captives in his train and gave gifts to men."* (Ephesians 4:8) This verse in Ephesians is quoting Psalm 68:18. This is a prophecy fulfilled in Jesus. Our Savior has freed us. Imagine Him storming the gates of hell, freeing the prisoners, and walking out with the keys of authority. All the captives the devil held in bondage are free and are following the Son into the Kingdom of Light. It's amazing!

All of this authority is only through Jesus, and not on our own. This is the reason that the gates of hell will not prevail against the Church. (See Mark 16:18). We are on the offense! We are to storm those gates of hell and take what the devil has stolen for the glory of God! Matthew

11:12 in the King James Version really describes vividly what the church of God is doing: *"And from the days of John the Baptist until now the kingdom of heaven suffereth violence, and the violent take it by force."* Don't be confused by the world violent, but try inserting "forceful" in for "violent", so that it reads, "the forceful take it by force." Wow! Jesus is the force in you.

At the end of Revelation, we read another verse regarding keys. It is the opposite of the verses we've been reading in that it refers to the keys to hell, instead of God's Kingdom.

> *Then I saw an angel coming down from heaven, having the key to the bottomless pit and a great chain in his hand.*
> Revelation 20:1 NKJV

This verse is the polar opposite of the previous verses. These keys are the keys to destruction and hell. The angel has given these keys to Satan and the keys to the kingdom to us! The door has been shut on Satan; his doom is sealed. Jesus has the keys to the kingdom and gives them to us to advance His kingdom.

Revelation 3:7 (NKJV) reads:

> *And to the angel of the church in Philadelphia write,*
> *"These things says He who is holy, He who is true, "He who has the key of David, He who opens and no one shuts, and shuts and no one opens"* . . .

This is the same thing Isaiah prophesied in the 22nd chapter of his book. Dare to believe God. Dare to believe that the Spirit of Jesus in you really is greater than he who is in the world. Nothing can stop you or stand against you when you really believe and live in that realm of faith and revelation. If God is for us, who can stand against us? Praise God, Jesus is Lord of all!

As we understand authority, we see that the reason the devil has authority to torment people in Hell is because they give him that authority by submitting to sin, and not to Christ. Once a person is submitted to Christ and His authority, Jesus gives that authority back to us to advance His kingdom. This is what happens at salvation. For God so loved the world, that He gave His only Son, that we may have salvation and authority to do His will. He can do all things without us, but chooses to work through us. How wonderful is our God!

CHAPTER 11

Experienced Theology

This chapter may not seem like it relates to the rest of the book at first, but please bear with us. It will make sense as you read on. The point is that any theology man makes about God needs to be backed up by experience. If your intellect has this grand way of thinking about God, but you don't actually experience what you've come up with (your theology), you need to question what is missing.

Many of our beliefs come from theology and tradition. Tradition is something we all kind of fall into, without even realizing it at times. The theology that we are taught and have heard becomes just one of those traditions. We really don't question it, because it has been passed down to us and has always been with us. Theology, however, is carnal. Webster's dictionary says theology means 1) the study of God and of God's relation to the world, and 2) a theological theory or system.

With this being the case, and the knowledge that things of men are at best imperfect, we ought to go by the Word of God - Holy Scripture! Sadly, sometimes we attempt to fit whatever our theology is into the Bible, instead of simply believing what the Bible says. We rationalize, and sometimes we even dismiss what the Bible says.

One day in 2007 a Pastor friend asked me (Kirk) if I'd like to go to the "W" at Mars Hill Bible Church in Michigan. He said it was just a meeting of people who liked to pray and really believed their prayers would be answered. I agreed to go, as I wasn't doing anything that evening anyway (see my excitement for prayer). We sang some praise songs and then listened to a teaching. I remember the teaching being on how the Bible was true, and how we could trust what it said. I'd have to say my mouth was hanging open with my chin on the ground for the whole meeting.

I had never heard teaching and praying like that! These people actually believed and really expected God to move when they prayed! He didn't disappoint either. People gave testimonies and others were healed during the meeting. I was witnessing the miraculous.

This has now become my experience with prayer. Unbelievable, miraculous things have been happening through my prayers. Not just once and a while either. I'm talking daily happenings.

I've gone into all this to show actual evidence that when I was following the teachings of man, the things of God were basically absent. My belief system was carnally conceived thoughts about God. These are deep intelligent thoughts in the natural realm, by very intelligent people, people who are much more intelligent than me. But they were still carnal. During this time of transition in my thoughts about God and the church, I went through a time of searching for truth.

The result of that search ended up being quite simple and ended where it started -in Holy Scripture. Specifically John 16:13a which says, *"When the Spirit of truth comes, He will guide you into all truth."* Yes I believe that the written (logos) Word is truth, and just as important is the spoken (rhema) Word. The spoken Spirit of Truth proceeds, or goes out from the Father (John 15:26) and guides us into all truth (John 16:13). Unless we have the written Word opened up to us by the Spirit of Truth, it's just a compilation of words in a dusty book.

Now, ponder this statement: "You can't make a theology of your experience."

This is a statement that was made during a discussion regarding the gifts of the Spirit. A pastor friend thought that the gift of the "word of knowledge" was something that gave a person a special ability to learn and remember facts and ideas learned through travel and experiences, as well as books and other media. I (Kirk) was telling him some of my experiences in using this gift. It has been my experience that the gift of the Word of Knowledge is when the Lord drops a Word of Knowledge about a person or situation into your spirit that you could not otherwise have known. That's when he stated, "You can't make a theology of your experience".

I forgot about that conversation until, while in prayer, it was again brought to my attention. It was like opening a can of worms. I started to receive verses and thoughts regarding this for the next week. These thoughts and verses were things I could have never thought of myself. I think they might be . . . shhhhh don't tell . . . words of knowledge!

The reason we bring this up is because it has to do with theology and our experience of theology. So first of all, what is theology? Merriam Webster says: "1 : the study of religious faith, practice, and experience; especially : the study of God and of God's relation to the world 2 a : a theological theory or system."

There it is, in the dictionary. It says that theology is an experience. You can't really have a theology without experience. Theology without experience is dead. Think of it! What does it mean to follow Christ if there is no experience? Even the Bible is just an old book with a lot of words until the Holy Spirit breathes life into it. After that, it becomes an experience. Without the experience of following Christ, we would just have religion or traditions. Or possibly something Kirk's son calls a "God fan club." It is like going to your favorite sporting event. It's exciting while you're there, but when you leave you haven't really been changed, the world hasn't changed, and you go on in life the same as before you ever attended the event. You are a fan, but your team winning or losing really has no lasting effect on you.

We did church like that for a lot of years (not being changed). But then after being baptized in the Holy Spirit, things were different. We experienced something profound and life changing. We couldn't go back to what we were before. Doing church didn't cut it anymore. We began to hear His voice, and see visions, as well as work in the gifts of the Spirit. We began to experience God! Our previous lives seem empty and boring, full of fear, striving and never really bringing satisfaction. I (Kirk) always thought people who spoke in tongues, saw visions, and heard God speak were a bunch of weirdos. Now I am one! Now we want to do whatever God wants us to do, and that can be scary.

We never want to go back. Living within God's will, hearing Him, and being obedient is exciting and each day is different. We have no idea what we will be asked to do next or where He is leading, but we trust Him implicitly. The Bible has come alive! The rules and legalism are gone, replaced by the law which is written on our hearts and in our minds. Our experience has been life changing and is affecting others around us now in ways that we never dreamed possible. Abundant life, anyone?

We say that we serve a risen Savior which is Christ the LORD; we say that we have a personal relationship with Him, right? This relationship could be with a rock if there is no experience! What is a relationship if there is no experience? Is God limited to simply operating in a person's mind? Is that what He wants?

For the word of God is living and active and sharper than any two-edged sword, and piercing as far as the division of soul and spirit, of both joints and marrow, and able to judge the thoughts and intentions of the heart. (Hebrews 4:12)

This passage from Hebrews sure sounds like an experience in the extreme! The Word of God should be an experience, whether it's studying the written word – the Bible, study of the Word Himself (Jesus Christ) or a spoken word (rhema) from the Holy Spirit. If the word were not living, we would be left with rituals, traditions, and religion. Surprisingly, those three things are exactly what some people settle for, and once ingrained into their lives, they actually desire this cheap imitation instead of the experience of God Himself. It's easy and comfortable for them: obey a few rules, show up on Sunday, look better than the guy next to them, etc. We've been there and done that. That is not experiencing God. That experience is similar to what the Israelites experienced after they went out of Egypt. They didn't want to go near God. They wanted Moses to do it for them. Moses got to experience God, and the people settled for less.

> *My prayer is not for them alone. I pray also for those who will believe in me through their message, that all of them may be one, Father, just as you are in me and I am in you. May they also be in us so that the world may believe that you have sent me. I have given them the glory that you gave me, that they may be one as we are one— I in them and you in me—so that they may be brought to complete unity. Then the world will know that you sent me and have loved them even as you have loved me.* (John 17:20-23)

If God is in us and we are one with God and with each other, we ought to be experiencing God. The world will know Jesus through experience with Jesus. *"I tell you the truth, we speak of what we know, and we testify to what we have seen, but still you people do not accept our testimony"* (John 3:11). Jesus made several statements indicating his knowledge of heavenly things, His experience. We too then should testify of our experience, imitating our LORD and Savior. This means that we should have a story to tell, an experience.

They overcame him by the blood of the Lamb and by the word of their testimony; they did not love their lives so much as to shrink from death. (Revelation 12:11)

The Word tells us that the way we overcome the accuser is by the blood of the Lamb and word of our testimony. We are to be fearless about this and not even shrink from death. Testimony must be pretty important then, especially if we are supposed to use it to overcome the enemy.

We should give our testimony in faith. When you see a miracle, believe it. Don't dismiss it. Why even pray, if we don't believe prayer is powerful and effective, and if we won't give God credit for moving when He does? Give praise when you see God move. Believe Him.

Don't be deceived, my dear brothers. Every good and perfect gift is from above, coming down from the Father of the heavenly lights, who does not change like shifting shadows. He chose to give us birth through the word of truth, that we might be a kind of first fruits of all he created.(James 1:16-18)

When we experience a gift (like healing) we should give complete thanks to God, and we should not weaken other people's faith by indicating that God doesn't really answer prayer or that He doesn't heal people, or that somehow a witnessed healing was a fluke. James has something to say about this.

But when he asks, he must believe and not doubt, because he who doubts is like a wave of the sea, blown and tossed by the wind. That man should not think he will receive anything from the Lord; he is a double-minded man, unstable in all he does. (James 1:6-8)

So, when we pray, we must not doubt or we can expect to receive nothing from the LORD. This means even after we have prayed, our testimony should be full of faith to believe that God has moved on our behalf. Why would we doubt this anyway? Are we trying to save others from having too much faith, so they aren't disappointed if their prayer doesn't end in a miracle? As the church, aren't we supposed to build each other's faith? We need to give testimony that is full of faith.

What would some of the experiences that God has for us look like? This is a very deep well. We'll list a few in addition to what is already written previously in this chapter.

First, God is love. God desires us to experience His love. John 3:16-21 says,

> For God so loved the world that he gave his one and only Son, that whoever believes in him shall not perish but have eternal life. For God did not send his Son into the world to condemn the world, but to save the world through him. Whoever believes in him is not condemned, but whoever does not believe stands condemned already because he has not believed in the name of God's one and only Son. This is the verdict: Light has come into the world, but men loved darkness instead of light because their deeds were evil. Everyone who does evil hates the light, and will not come into the light for fear that his deeds will be exposed. But whoever lives by the truth comes into the light, so that it may be seen plainly that what he has done has been done through God.

What an awesome God we serve! He didn't even spare His own Son in order that we could experience salvation and a relationship with Him. All we must do is believe on Him, and we are not condemned. It's simple. God loves us so much, that there is no way this deep, deep love is only for the intellect. You only have to take a look around you to see that there is beauty everywhere in nature, no matter where you are. We can experience love from a parent, a husband or wife, friend, or even a complete stranger. We are supposed to love and be loved - it's how we were created. No matter how much love we have experienced in the natural world though, God loves us more! He wants to show His love to you. Believe on His Son, ask the Holy Spirit to come into you, then ask God to show you His love. Your life will never be the same, and you'll never want to go back to who you were.

Secondly, God is forgiving. Have you experienced forgiveness? *"If we confess our sins, he is faithful and just and will forgive us our sins and purify us from all unrighteousness"* (John 1:9). We confess, repent (turn away from sin), and forgiveness is ours. This is real forgiveness. It brings an end to guilt, shame and fear. We are able to experience freedom through Jesus Christ. Again, this is an experience. Luke 24:46-48 says,

> *He told them, "This is what is written: The Christ will suffer and rise from the dead on the third day, and repentance and forgiveness of sins will be preached in his name to all nations, beginning at Jerusalem. You are witnesses of these things."*

Experience the forgiveness and then go and be a witness.

Thirdly, we ought to experience all the promises of God in the Word. *"For all the promises of God in Him are Yes, and in Him Amen, to the glory of God through us"* (2 Corinthians 1:20). If God makes a promise in His Word, that promise is fulfilled through Jesus Christ. In Christ the answer is "yes!"

> *Surely he took up our infirmities and carried our sorrows,*
> *yet we considered him stricken by God,*
> *smitten by him, and afflicted.*
> *But he was pierced for our transgressions,*
> *he was crushed for our iniquities;*
> *the punishment that brought us peace was upon him,*
> *and by his wounds we are healed.* (Isaiah 53:4-5)

This passage of Isaiah is a promise of God. It tells us what Jesus accomplished on the cross. Our faith in what Jesus has done brings that experience to life. Peter writes about the experience of healing in one of his letters. *"He himself bore our sins in his body on the tree, so that we might die to sins and live for righteousness; by his wounds you have been healed"* (1 Peter 2:24). Healing is an experience from the atonement that Jesus brought to everyone who asked him throughout the New Testament. These people experienced Jesus through healing. People healed through the laying on of hands still experience Him today because He doesn't change. He is the same yesterday, today, and forever. What He did then, He does now.

> *Is any one of you sick? He should call the elders of the church to pray over him and anoint him with oil in the name of the Lord. And the prayer offered in faith will make the sick person well; the Lord will raise him up. If he has sinned, he will be forgiven. Therefore confess your sins to each other and pray for each other so that you may be healed. The prayer of a righteous man is powerful and effective.* (James 5:14-16)

Is healing our experience? According to the Word it should be. Therefore, our theology/ experience should line up with the Word. Satan is here to kill, steal and destroy. He is the father of lies. So, when we ask for healing, what we are really asking for is the manifestation of that healing because healing was accomplished by Jesus on the cross. Jesus said, "It is finished." Christ has already paid for healing in full, the same as He has born all of our sin. It's a done deal. We receive it through faith.

We need faith to bring these promises of God into the natural realm. This brings us to the fourth experience we want to address. Faith. What is faith? *"Now faith is being sure of what we hope for and certain of what we do not see"* (Hebrews 11:1). Faith is being fully persuaded that God will do what He says. The Amplified version of the Bible describes faith well. *"Now faith is the assurance (the confirmation, the title deed) of the things [we] hope for, being the proof of things [we] do not see and the conviction of their reality [faith perceiving as real fact what is not revealed by the senses]."* (Hebrews 11:1) This means, we believe even when our eyes do not show us what we're believing for. Everything in the natural may look one way, when God says it is another way. We are to believe God, not what our eyes see. This is faith.

Hebrews chapter 11 lists many people who had faith, even though what their eyes saw told them a different story. We are to be like these people, and believe the Word of God and speak the Word of God over our situations until the natural lines up with the spiritual. A great example of this is when God changed Abram's name to Abraham. He was calling Abraham the father of many nations long before it was a reality. God actually made Abraham call himself the father of many nations. Abraham spoke the Truth over his life and it eventually manifested in the natural realm.

Faith is when we come to the point where we realize that the Word of God really is the absolute truth and that the only way to receive this truth is to depend on the Holy Spirit (the Spirit of truth) to lead us into all truth. Then being certain of what we do not see really becomes a fact in our lives.

> *I have much more to say to you, more than you can now bear. But when he, the Spirit of truth, comes, he will guide you into all truth. He will not speak on his own; he will speak only what he hears, and he will tell you what is yet to come. He will bring glory to me by taking from what is mine and making it known to you. All that belongs to the Father is mine. That is why I said the Spirit will take from what is mine and make it known to you.* (John 16:12-15)

It is the Spirit that leads us into all Truth, and it is the Spirit that we need to believe, not the world, the devil, or even our own eyes.

Finally, we want to address the experience of praise. Much can be, and has been, written about this topic. Praise is incredibly powerful. It defeats the darkness and draws us into the presence of the King. *"But You are holy, O*

You Who dwell in [the holy place where] the praises of Israel [are offered] (Psalm 22:3, AMP). God actually inhabits our praises. That is power, and that is experience! We are called to worship God, and we should want to worship God. When you are in a place where you really don't feel like worshipping and praising, that's when you need to do it most. Offer a sacrifice of praise. *"But you are a chosen people, a royal priesthood, a holy nation, a people belonging to God, that you may declare the praises of him who called you out of darkness into his wonderful light"* (1 Peter 2:9).

Remember what God has done for you, and praise Him for it. Can there be any darkness where there is His light? God obviously wants to be praised, and we are made to do that. He says to worship Him in "spirit and in truth" (John 4:24). So praise Him, and watch the darkness leave, and enjoy the experience of praise with God.

These are just a few ways we are to experience our God. We could never run out of ways to experience our infinite God. Try using your five natural senses sometime. Imagine yourself walking with Him in the cool of the garden like Adam and Eve did at first. Come into the pure light, speak to your Father, let Him love you, and love Him back. Experience life in its fullest where there is no darkness.

The LORD could have made us all like robots without free will – without the freedom to choose whether we would choose to experience Him. But, that's not what He wanted. He wanted people who had the freedom to choose not to love Him, to make the choice to love Him. He wanted you.

Now what I am commanding you today is not too difficult for you or beyond your reach. It is not up in heaven, so that you have to ask, "Who will ascend into heaven to get it and proclaim it to us so we may obey it?" Nor is it beyond the sea, so that you have to ask, "Who will cross the sea to get it and proclaim it to us so we may obey it?" No, the word is very near you; it is in your mouth and in your heart so you may obey it.

See, I set before you today life and prosperity, death and destruction. For I command you today to love the LORD your God, to walk in his ways, and to keep his commands, decrees and laws; then you will live and increase, and the LORD your God will bless you in the land you are entering to possess.

But if your heart turns away and you are not obedient, and if you are drawn away to bow down to other gods and worship them, I declare to you this day that you will certainly be destroyed. You will not live long in the land you are crossing the Jordan to enter and possess.

This day I call heaven and earth as witnesses against you that I have set before you life and death, blessings and curses. Now choose life, so that you and your children may live and that you may love the LORD your God, listen to his voice, and hold fast to him. For the LORD is your life, *and he will give you many years in the land he swore to give to your fathers, Abraham, Isaac and Jacob.*
Deuteronomy 30:11-16

This scripture from Deuteronomy is still true, with the difference being that we live now after God has released us from the law of sin and death (Romans 8:2) and now we must follow after, and believe on Christ Jesus. Once again, He (Jesus) is perfect theology. The perfect representation of God (Hebrews 1:3) is not a theological theory or a study of God by men, He is God Himself. He is living and active, and wants to have a relationship with everyone (John 3:16, John 16:12-15, John 12:32). He loves us, and He calls everyone to Himself. We have no excuse. Will we accept the gift He wants so much to give us? Will we experience our theology?

Recommended Reading: *A Heart Ablaze* by John Bevere

APPENDIX A

Salvation Prayer

I f you have never believed and confessed Jesus as your Savior and Lord and would like to do it, we would like to offer this prayer for you to pray. Please remember this is a serious commitment. This is not a mental consent, but a deep heart belief that Jesus is Savior and Jesus is Lord. There is no other name under heaven by which we may be saved.

Heavenly Father,
I confess that I have lived for myself and right now I desire to live for you. I believe that Jesus is the only begotten Son of God and the Savior of the world. I believe your Word is Truth and I desire to live by it. So, today _____ *(fill in date), I confess Jesus as my Lord and Savior and I renounce all deeds of darkness. I desire to live for you and not myself.*
Thank you, Lord. My life is complete in You!

Congratulations! The Word says there is rejoicing in heaven over one sinner who repents! We now encourage you to be baptized and filled with the Holy Spirit as in the book of Acts and to join with other brothers and sisters in Christ through a local church body who believe the full gospel message.

Holy Spirit Filling Prayer

After salvation (see Appendix A), the Lord says to join with him through water baptism (a sign of repentance). We encourage you to be baptized in water as a sign of your salvation. Hebrews 6:2 talks about baptisms (plural) being an elementary teaching. We receive a water baptism, where we go under the water and die to self (flesh) and come out of the water and rise to new life in Christ. We are Born Again! However, this appendix addresses the baptism of the Holy Spirit.

It is clear from scripture and evidenced in real lives today that there is a separate baptism commonly called Baptism of the Holy Spirit. It is with this baptism that we receive power from the Holy Spirit to do the works of God, such as those listed in Mark 16 (healing the sick, raising the dead, casting out demons, etc.).

Matthew 3:11 *I baptize you with water for repentance. But after me will come one who is more powerful than I, whose sandals I am not fit to carry. He will baptize you with the Holy Spirit and with fire.*

Acts 1:5 *"For John baptized with water, but in a few days you will be baptized with the Holy Spirit."*

Peter recalls this after he visits Cornelius' house and talks to the other leaders of the church. He says, *"Then I remembered the word of the Lord, how He said, 'John indeed baptized with water, but you shall be baptized with the Holy Spirit.'"*

Acts 1:8 *"But you will receive power when the Holy Spirit comes on you; and you will be my witnesses in Jerusalem, and in all Judea and Samaria, and to the ends of the earth."*

The Holy Spirit came to the believers at Pentecost and then it was passed on through the laying on of hands and/or prayer, generally. This is how God usually works within the church. He wants us to go and preach the gospel. He wants us to heal the sick and raise the dead. He wants us to cleanse the lepers and cast out demons. He wants us to give to the poor and visit those in prison. He wants us to baptize in the name of Jesus for salvation and for the empowerment of the Holy Spirit.

Acts 2:1-4 *When the day of Pentecost came, they were all together in one place. Suddenly a sound like the blowing of a violent wind came from heaven and filled the whole house where they were sitting. They saw what seemed to be tongues of fire that separated and came to rest on each of them. All of them were filled with the Holy Spirit and began to speak in other tongues as the Spirit enabled them.*

Acts 2:17-18 *"In the last days, God says,*
I will pour out my Spirit on all people.
Yours sons and daughters will prophesy,
your young men will see visions,
your old men will dream dreams.
Even on my servants, both men and women,
I will pour out my Spirit in those days,
and they will prophesy." (Joel 2:28-32)

Acts 2:33 *Exalted to the right hand of God, he has received from the Father the promised Holy Spirit and has poured out what you now see and hear.*

Acts 6:3-5 *"Brothers, choose seven men from among you who are known to be full of the Spirit and wisdom. We will turn this responsibility over to them and give our attention to prayer and the ministry of the word." This proposal pleased the whole group. They chose Stephen, a man full of faith and of the Holy Spirit; also Philip, Procorus, Nicanor, Timon, Parmenas, and Nicolas from Antioch, a convert to Judaism.*

"Among you" means believers (saved). If all had equal filling of the Holy Spirit, there would be no point to saying "full of the Spirit and wisdom." You must be saved first in order to receive the Holy Spirit baptism.

Acts 7:55 *But Stephen, full of the Holy Spirit, looked up to heaven and saw the glory of God, and Jesus standing at the right hand of God.*

Acts 8:9-24 *Now for some time a man Simon had practiced sorcery in the city and amazed all the people of Samaria. He boasted that he was someone great, and all the people, both high and low, gave him their attention and exclaimed, "This man is the divine power known as the Great Power." They followed him because he had amazed them for a long time with his magic. But when they believed Philip as he preached the good news of the kingdom of God and the name of Jesus Christ, they were baptized, both men and women. Simon himself believed and was baptized. And he followed Philip everywhere, astonished by the great signs and miracles he saw. When the apostles in Jerusalem heard that Samaria had accepted the word of God, they sent Peter and John to them. When they arrived, they prayed for them that they might receive the Holy Spirit, because the Holy Spirit had not yet come upon any of them; they had simply been baptized into the name of the Lord Jesus. Then Peter and John placed their hands on them, and they received the Holy Spirit. When Simon saw that the Spirit was given at the laying on of the apostles' hands, he offered them* *money and said, "Give me also this ability so that everyone on whom I lay my hands may receive the Holy Spirit." Peter answered: "May your money perish with you, because you thought you could buy the gift of God with money! You have no part or share in this ministry, because you heart is not right before God. Repent of this wickedness and pray to the Lord. Perhaps he will forgive you for having such a thought in your heart. For I see that you are full of bitterness and captive to sin." Then Simon answered, "Pray to the Lord for me so that nothing you have said may happen to me."*

There's a lot going on here. . .
Obviously, these people believed in Jesus (were saved), but they hadn't received empowerment from the Holy Spirit until Peter and John came.

Acts 8:18-24 *When Simon saw that the Spirit was given at the laying on of the apostles' hands, he offered them money and said, "Give me also this ability so that everyone on whom I lay my hands may receive the Holy Spirit." Peter answered: "May your money perish with you, because you thought you could buy the gift of God with money! You have no part or share in this ministry, because your heart is not right before God. Repent of this wickedness and pray to the Lord. Perhaps he will forgive you for having such a thought in your heart. For I see that you are full of bitterness and captive to sin." Then Simon answered, "Pray to the Lord for me so that nothing you have said may happen to me."*

Simon saw the difference that happened in a people's lives who received the baptism of the Holy Spirit and he wanted it. We should have such power in our lives that others want it!

Acts 9:17 *Then Ananias went to the house and entered it. Placing his hands on Saul, he said, "Brother Saul, the Lord – Jesus, who appeared to you on the road as you were coming here – has sent me so that you may see again and be filled with the Holy Spirit." Immediately, something like scales fell from Saul's eyes, and he could see again. He got up and was baptized, and after taking some food, he regained his strength.*

Here Paul was converted on the road to Damascus. However, he didn't receive the Holy Spirit until Ananias came. Ananias addresses Paul as "brother" before baptizing him in the Holy Spirit, yet another indication he was saved already. In this case, water baptism came after Holy Spirit baptism.

Acts 10:44-48 *While Peter was still speaking these words, the Holy Spirit came on all who heard the message. The circumcised believers who had come with Peter were astonished that the gift of the Holy Spirit had been poured out even on the Gentiles. For they heard them speaking in tongues and praising God. Then Peter said, "Can anyone keep these people from being baptized with water? They have received the Holy Spirit just as we have." So he ordered that they be baptized in the name of Jesus Christ. Then they asked Peter to stay with them for a few days.*

This is Cornelius' house that Peter is at. Cornelius was a Gentile who feared God, who prayed, and gave to the poor. When God told Cornelius to send for Peter so he could explain the way of salvation to him, Cornelius invited his relatives and close friends. As Peter gave the message of Jesus Christ, they were all baptized in the Holy Spirit and the manifestation of it was that they spoke in tongues. Peter was amazed that even Gentiles would be eligible for this gift of God.

The whole of Acts 10 talks of Cornelius' household. Cornelius was saved. Verse 36 says that he knew. But God sent Peter to more clearly explain and to baptize them and because He wanted to baptize them in the Holy Spirit. This was possibly as much a revelation and powerful experience for Cornelius, his household, and close friends, as it was for Peter and the circumcised Jews who came with him.

Acts 11:15-16 (Peter explains to the apostles what happened at Cornelius' house) *"As I began to speak, the Holy Spirit came on them as he had come on us at the beginning* [Pentecost]. *Then I remembered what the Lord had said: 'John baptized with water, but you will be baptized with the Holy*

Spirit.' So if God gave them the same gift as he gave us, who believed in the Lord Jesus Christ, who was I to think that I could oppose God?"

Acts 18:24-25 *Meanwhile a Jew named Apollos, a native of Alexandria, came to Ephesus. He was a learned man, with a thorough knowledge of the Scriptures. He had been instructed in the way of the Lord, and he spoke with great fervor and taught about Jesus accurately, though he knew only the baptism of John.*

This shows that even without the baptism of the Holy Spirit we can do good for the Kingdom, but with it, we can do even more.

Acts 19:1-6 *While Apollos was at Corinth, Paul took the road through the interior and arrived at Ephesus. There he found some disciples and asked them, "Did you receive the Holy Spirit when you believed?" They answered, "No, we have not even heard that there is a Holy Spirit." So Paul asked, "Then what baptism did you receive?" "John's baptism," they replied. Paul said, John's baptism was a baptism of repentance. He told the people to believe in the one coming after him, that is, in Jesus." On hearing this, they were baptized into the name of the Lord Jesus. When Paul placed his hands on them, the Holy Spirit came on them, and they spoke in tongues and prophesied. There were about twelve men in all.*

Obviously, if they are questioned about Holy Spirit baptism, it is important. There is an obvious contrast between water (repentance) baptism and Holy Spirit baptism. These men were believers. They were saved, but they needed the baptism of the Holy Spirit for empowerment. Once again the Spirit comes and gives tongues as evidence of it.

John 1:32-34 (John the Baptist is speaking here.) *Then John gave this testimony: "I saw the Spirit come down from heaven as a dove and remain on him. I would not have known him, except that the one who sent me to baptize with water told me, 'The man on whom you see the Spirit come* *down and remain is he who will baptize with the Holy Spirit'. I have seen and I testify that his is the Son of God."*

Ephesians 1:13-14 *And you also were included in Christ when you heard the word of truth, the gospel of your salvation. Having believed, you were marked in him with a seal, the promised Holy Spirit, who is a deposit guaranteeing our inheritance until the redemption of those who are God's possession – to the praise of his glory.*

We all receive the Spirit guaranteeing our inheritance when we believe. It's the baptism of the Holy Spirit that brings fullness, however. We are influenced by the Holy Spirit when we become believers, but we are indwelt with Him when we are baptized into the Holy Spirit.

Why do we need the baptism of the Holy Spirit? For the gifts, for the edification of the body (church), edification of ourselves, and as a sign to unbelievers.

Tongues will come with the baptism of the Holy Spirit. There are three kinds of tongues we notice in the Word. One is speaking in tongues of the earth that are unknown to the speaker. This is so the hearers can hear the word of God, like at Pentecost. (1 Cor 14:22) Another is a personal prayer language. The third is speaking in a heavenly tongue in public, after which someone will give the interpretation (1 Cor 12:10), so the body of believers is edified. This is similar to prophecy.

The point in the Bible where God says, "Do all speak with tongues?" is not referring to our personal prayer language, but instead to the ministry gift of speaking in tongues or interpreting. Not everyone operates in the ministry gifts listed in 1 Cor 12:28-30 all the time, though God will use a Spirit-filled believer to operate in all the gifts from time to time as He sees fit. That doesn't mean, however, that because God uses you to prophecy at some point, that you hold the office of a prophet, etc.

John Bevere in *Drawing Near* gives a good explanation of the differences between tongues and I quote here some of what he says.

> . . . *Paul is speaking about ministry giftings that God has set in the church* [in 1 Cor 12:28-30]. *Certainly* not all *are apostles, or prophets, or teachers, or pastors, or have gifts of miracles and healings, and all* do not *have the ministry gift of speaking in tongues or interpretation of heavenly tongues. Why is that? The answer is found in the following:*

> *Therefore tongues* [tongues for a sign] *are for a sign, not to those who believe but to unbelievers . . . if the whole church comes together in one place, and all speak with tongues* [tongues for interpretation], *and there comes in those who are uninformed or unbelievers, will they not say that you are out of your mind? (I Cor. 14:22-23,* author's emphasis*)*

> *Before I* [John Bevere] *answer our question, let me point out that these two verses clearly show the difference between the two public tongues. He* [Paul] *first writes that tongues are a sign to unbelievers. This is speaking languages of this earth in which we have never been trained. An unbeliever who knows these languages clearly sees that there is no possible way we could speak those words except by miraculous intervention of the Lord. So it is a sign to the unbeliever.*

> *Then Paul talks about the whole church coming together and speaking in tongues at the same time. This is clearly the tongues that are the languages of heaven. The reason I know this is that all the disciples on the day of Pentecost were all speaking in different earthly languages the wonderful works of God. They did not have to be interpreted, for the unbelievers knew what they were saying. He is talking in this verse about speaking to the church in the heavenly tongue that needs to be interpreted. If not, then no*

one would understand. As you can see, there is no need for all to
speak in tongues otherwise the uninformed or unbelievers would
think we were crazy.

So the answer to this question "Do all speak in tongues?" which
has been so misunderstood by many, is simple. God is selective
when it comes to ministry gifts He places in the church, because
not all need to operate in it. But He is not partial, and I repeat,
He is not selective, in what He gives to each of us believers for our
own personal walk.
(p. 174-175)

So we see that there are at least three different kinds of tongues, but each Spirit-filled believer will have at least their own personal tongue for personal prayer. Jude tells us that praying in our prayer language will build us up, or edify us in our spirit (Jude 20-21). We can use our prayer language to pray when we don't know what to pray, either for ourselves or for others. (See Romans 8:6-27.)

First Corinthians 14 talks about speaking and praying in tongues. Paul (through the Holy Spirit) says, "For anyone who speaks in a tongue does not speak to men but to God. Indeed no one understands him; he utters mysteries with his spirit." This is obviously not referring to speaking in the kind of tongues we read about at Pentecost because those were languages of the world, unknown to the speakers, and those around them understood it. No, the tongues Paul is describing here are the personal tongues God gives us that only God understands.

Why would God want us praying in a language no one understands? There are several reasons, and we don't pretend to know all the answers. However, one reason is because we don't always know how to pray (Rom 8). Additionally, the devil can't understand what we're praying when the Holy Spirit gives us a language from heaven to pray.

Since we don't know what we're praying, we're told that we're able to ask for the interpretation. Paul writes, "For this reason anyone who speaks in a tongue should pray that he may interpret what he says. For if I pray in a tongue, my spirit prays, but my mind is unfruitful." (1 Cor 14:13-14).

When we're praying in tongues, we're not speaking to men, like tongues for interpretation, but we're speaking to God. First Corinthians 14:2 reads, *"For anyone who speaks in a tongue does not speak to men but to God. Indeed, no one understands him; he utters mysteries with his spirit."* This is what the Psalmist meant when he said "deep calls to deep" (Psalm 42:7). Our spirits join with God's Spirit and we call out to each other as we pray in tongues.

Isaiah even prophecied about tongues when he wrote, *". . . with foreign lips and strange tongues God will speak to this people, to whom he said, 'This is the resting place, let the weary rest'; and, 'This is the place of repose'"* (Isaiah 28:11-12). The Holy Spirit speaks in a foreign tongue through us and in that we find rest.

Why is it that some of the body of Christ fights the baptism of the Holy Spirit and speaking in tongues? Part of the answer is that the devil fears it. He knows the baptism of the Holy Spirit brings power and revelation, and he knows that praying in tongues is secret communication with the King that also brings power and revelation, as well as rest. One of the other reasons, we believe is that we get prideful that we have all the answers and won't change our minds know matter what is revealed. The following is a quote from John Bevere in *Drawing Near:* "One of the greatest tragedies I have observed in my years of ministry is that so many Christians interpret the Word of God through their experiences, rather than allowing the Word of God to dictate their experiences." (p. 180) This is a tragedy indeed.

Yet another reason to pray in tongues is to build up our inner person. Paul tells us this in 1 Corinthians 14:4, *"He who speaks in a tongue edifies himself . . .".* Jude also tells us this is a reason to pray in tongues: *"But you, dear friends, build yourselves up in your most holy faith and pray in the Holy Spirit."*

Acts 4:31 *After they prayed, the place where they were meeting was shaken. And they were all filled with the Holy Spirit and spoke the word of God boldly.* This happened after the religious leaders had put Peter and John in jail and angels came and let them out. It says that after prayer, they (the apostles and disciples of Christ) where filled with the Holy Spirit, but this was quite a while after their baptism of the Holy Spirit. So, it indicates that we can get more of the HS. The Spirit is so great, we can't contain all of Him. We just keep getting more and maybe even losing some as we go away from God and then get more refilling, etc. However, the baptism we never lose because it's for empowerment and the gifts of God are irrevocable.

We all receive the Spirit guaranteeing our inheritance when we believe. It's the baptism of the Holy Spirit that brings fullness, however.

Why do we need the baptism of the Holy Spirit? For the gifts, for the edification of the body, and as a sign to unbelievers.

If you would like to receive the baptism of the Holy Spirit, you can ask a spirit-filled believer to lay hands on you and pray for you to receive it. Or, you can pray the prayer below and receive it on your own.

Jesus,
I come before you and ask for the filling of the Holy Spirit. I want to operate in the gifts and do the works you've prepared for me to do. Fill me now, I pray!

Congratulations! God says the gates of hell will not prevail against His Church!

ABOUT THE AUTHORS

Tiffany Root is passionate about seeing people set free in Christ Jesus. She is the co-leader of Seeking the Glory of God, a ministry where she teaches and leads in prayer. She has also led worship services and prayer meetings at her church and in other venues. She is also involved with the Healing Rooms in Grandville, Michigan. In the past, Tiffany taught High School English, and now currently homeschools. Tiffany lives in Byron Center, Michigan with her husband, Joel, and three children, Kaylee, William, and Lydia.

Kirk VandeGuchte loves the LORD and wants to share a journey of finding the truth. Kirk co-leads Seeking the Glory of God with Tiffany Root, has led worship services and prayer meetings at various churches, and has also been involved with various prayer ministries at other locations including the Healing Rooms of Grand Rapids, the Healing Rooms of Grandville, and the "W" at Mars Hill Bible Church. Kirk attended Spartan School of Aeronautics, graduated in 1979 and has been working in the aviation industry for a little over 30 years. He is currently employed as an Aviation Maintenance Tech., working on corporate aircraft. Kirk is married to and is desperately in love with his wife Barb. They reside in Byron Center, Michigan, have three sons, one daugther-in-law, and one granddaughter.